# Find us online

## > GOV.UK – Simpler, clearer, faster

GOV.UK is the best place to find government services and information for

- car drivers
- motorcyclists
- driving licences
- driving and riding tests
- towing a caravan or trailer
- medical rules
- driving and riding for a living
- online services.

Visit **www.gov.uk and try it out!**

You can also find contact details for DSA and other motoring agencies like DVLA at **www.gov.uk**

You'll notice that links to **GOV.UK**, the UK's new central government site, don't always take you to a specific page. This is because this new kind of site constantly adapts to what people really search for and so such static links would quickly go out of date. Try it out. Simply search what you need from your preferred search site or from **www.gov.uk** and you should find what you're looking for. You can give feedback to the Government Digital Service from the website.

# Driving Standards Agency

The Driving Standards Agency (DSA) is an executive agency of the Department for Transport. You'll see its logo at theory and practical test centres.

DSA aims to promote road safety through the advancement of driving standards, by

- establishing and developing high standards and best practice in driving and riding on the road; before people start to drive, as they learn, and after they pass their test
- ensuring high standards of instruction for different types of driver and rider
- conducting the statutory theory and practical tests efficiently, fairly and consistently across the country
- providing a centre of excellence for driver training and driving standards
- developing a range of publications and other publicity material designed to promote safe riding for life.

The Driving Standards Agency recognises and values its customers. It will treat all its customers with respect, and deliver its services in an objective, polite and fair way.

**www.gov.uk/dsa**

The Driver and Vehicle Agency (DVA) is an executive agency within the Department of the Environment for Northern Ireland.

Its primary aim is to promote and improve road safety through the advancement of driving standards and implementation of the government's policies for improving the mechanical standards of vehicles.

**dvani.gov.uk**

Driving
Standards
Agency

# The **OFFICIAL DSA GUIDE** to
# LEARNING
# TO RIDE

London: TSO

Written and compiled by the Learning Materials section of the Driving Standards Agency.

Published with the permission of the Driving Standards Agency on behalf of the Controller of Her Majesty's Stationery Office.

© Crown Copyright 2012

Previously known as *Official Motorcycling – CBT, theory & practical test*
First published 1998
Fourth edition 2003

New title – *The Official DSA Guide to Learning to Ride*
Fifth edition 2005
Sixth edition 2008
Seventh edition 2009
Eighth edition 2011
Ninth edition 2012
Second impression 2013

ISBN  978 011 553254 2

A CIP catalogue record for this book is available from the British Library.

**Other titles in the Driving Skills series**

*The Official DSA Guide to Driving – the essential skills*
*The Official DSA Theory Test for Car Drivers*
*The Official DSA Theory Test for Car Drivers (DVD-ROM)*
*The Official DSA Guide to Learning to Drive*
*Prepare for your Practical Driving Test DVD*
*DSA Driving Theory Quiz DVD*
*The Official Highway Code Interactive CD-ROM*

*The Official DSA Theory Test iPhone App*
*The Official DSA Theory Test Kit iPhone App*
*The Official Highway Code iPhone App*

*The Official DSA Guide to Riding – the essential skills*
*The Official DSA Theory Test for Motorcyclists*
*The Official DSA Theory Test for Motorcyclists (DVD-ROM)*
*Better Biking – the official DSA training aid (DVD)*

*The Official DSA Guide to Driving Buses and Coaches*
*The Official DSA Guide to Driving Goods Vehicles*
*The Official DSA Theory Test for Drivers of Large Vehicles*
*The Official DSA Theory Test for Drivers of Large Vehicles (CD-ROM)*
*Driver CPC – the official DSA guide for professional bus and coach drivers*
*Driver CPC – the official DSA guide for professional goods vehicle drivers*

*The Official DSA Guide to Tractor and Specialist Vehicle Driving Tests*

*The Official DSA Guide to Hazard Perception (DVD)*

100% recycled
This book is printed
on 100% recycled paper

**We're turning over a new leaf.**

RECYCLED
Paper made from
recycled material
FSC® C002151
www.fsc.org

# Contents

## 01 Getting started

| | |
|---|---|
| Message from the chief driving examiner | 9 |
| About this book | 10 |
| What is CBT? | 12 |
| The CBT course | 13 |
| Approved training bodies | 14 |
| Your motorcycle licence | 16 |

## 02 Compulsory basic training

| | |
|---|---|
| Element A – Introduction to CBT | 25 |
| Element B – Practical on-site training | 29 |
| Element C – Practical on-site riding | 35 |
| Element D – Practical on-road training | 45 |
| Element E – Practical on-road riding | 57 |
| CBT record | 67 |
| After CBT | 68 |

## 03 Before your tests

| | |
|---|---|
| Booking your tests | 71 |
| Your theory test | 73 |
| Theory into practice | 75 |
| The practical tests | 76 |
| Your test motorcycle | 79 |

## 04 The practical riding test off-road module

| | |
|---|---|
| The off-road module | 81 |
| The off-road manoeuvring area | 82 |
| Before you start the engine | 83 |
| Using the stand and manual handling | 84 |
| Slalom and figure of eight | 85 |
| Slow ride | 86 |
| U-turn | 87 |
| Cornering and controlled stopping | 88 |
| Cornering and the emergency stop | 89 |
| Cornering and the avoidance exercise | 90 |
| Other machines | 91 |

## 05 The practical riding test on-road module

| | |
|---|---|
| The on-road module | 93 |
| The eyesight test | 95 |
| Safety checks and balance question | 96 |
| The motorcycle controls | 98 |
| Moving off | 100 |
| Rear observation | 101 |
| Giving signals | 102 |
| Acting on signs and signals | 103 |
| Use of speed | 104 |
| Making progress | 105 |
| Hazards – the correct routine | 106 |
| Junctions and roundabouts | 107 |

## 05 The practical riding test on-road module contd

Overtaking 109
Meeting and passing other vehicles 110
Crossing the path of other vehicles 111
Following behind at a safe distance 112
Positioning and lane discipline 114
Pedestrian crossings 115
Selecting a safe place to stop 116
Awareness and anticipation 117
Independent riding 118
If you don't pass 120
If you pass both modules 121

## 06 Retesting

New Drivers Act 123
The extended test 124

## 07 Further information

Recommended syllabus 127

# section **one**
# GETTING STARTED

This section covers
- About this book
- What is CBT?
- The CBT course
- Approved training bodies
- Your motorcycle licence

# Message from the chief driving examiner

While riding a moped or motorcycle is fun and can help reduce congestion, riders have to remember how vulnerable they are on the road.

Over the years, various pieces of legislation have been introduced to reduce moped and motorcycle rider casualties, including the compulsory wearing of safety helmets, restrictions on the size of motorcycle that a learner can ride and the requirement for all learner riders to pass a theory test.

Compulsory basic training (CBT) was introduced in 1990 to equip new riders with basic skills before riding unaccompanied on the road. CBT isn't a test and there's no exam – it's a course of training you're required to complete satisfactorily. As a road safety initiative it has proved to be a great success.

On the other hand, the purpose of the practical test modules is to prove that you can ride your motorcycle safely on the road. During your practical test modules your examiner will want to see you riding to the standards set in this book.

Those riding standards are given here in an easy-to-read style with illustrations which explain simply what's required.

However, riding is never predictable. Road conditions or circumstances will demand that you use your initiative or common sense. You should be able to assess any situation and apply the guidance given in this book.

You shouldn't assume that if you pass your tests you're a good rider with nothing more to learn. Learning to ride a motorcycle is a continuous process, and the tests are just one stage in your riding career.

Make sure that your aim is always 'Safe riding for life'.

**Lesley Young**
Chief Driving Examiner

9

# About this book

Sections 1 and 2 of this book are designed to help you get the most out of the CBT course. Refer to them as you progress through each element and they'll help you gain a better understanding of what you need to achieve. The other sections will help you learn to ride competently and prepare for and pass your practical motorcycle test modules.

## Important factors

You're just beginning your motorcycling career and this book is only one of the important factors in your training. Other factors you need to consider include

- finding a good trainer
- adopting a positive attitude
- patience and practice.

How you choose to develop as a motorcyclist is up to you. You should aim to be a safe and confident rider for life. Don't just put on a show for your test and then revert to a lower standard. Take pride in always setting a good example.

*CBT will give you the basic skills you need to begin riding safely on the road.*

### How will each section of this book help me?

**Section 1** Outlines the five elements of the CBT course and tells you what you need to know about your motorcycle licence.

**Section 2** Explains the details of each element of the CBT course.

**Section 3** Contains advice on how to continue your training after CBT and tells you what you need to do before the test.

**Section 4** Details the requirements of the off-road module of the motorcycle test and gives simple, clear advice.

**Section 5** Details the on-road module of the motorcycle test and gives advice whether you pass or fail.

**Section 6** Gives details about the extended test for disqualified riders.

**Section 7** Details the recommended syllabus.

## Books to help you study

The official DSA range will provide you with a sound knowledge of riding skills and safe riding practices.

**The Official DSA Theory Test for Motorcyclists** This contains official revision theory test questions for motorcyclists including thorough explanations of the answers.

**The Official DSA Guide to Riding – the essential skills** This is the official reference book, giving practical advice and best practice for all riders.

**The Official Highway Code** (2007 edition) Essential reading for all road users. This updated edition contains the very latest rules of the road, up-to-date legislation and provides advice on road safety and best practice. It's also available on CD-ROM and as an eBook and iPhone app.

**Know Your Traffic Signs** This contains the vast majority of signs and road markings that you're likely to encounter.

The information in these books will be relevant throughout your riding life so make sure that you always have an up-to-date copy to which you can refer.

## Other media

**The Official DSA Theory Test for Motorcyclists (DVD-ROM)** This provides an interactive way of learning. You can also practise taking a mock theory test.

**The Official DSA Guide to Hazard Perception (DVD)** DSA strongly recommends that you use this, preferably with your instructor, to prepare for the hazard perception part of the test. The DVD is packed with useful tips, quizzes and expert advice. It also includes interactive hazard perception clips, and your performance will receive a score so you'll know if you're ready to pass.

**Better Biking – the official DSA training aid (DVD)** Expert advice on improving your skills and post-test rider training.

You can buy official DSA learning materials online at **tsoshop.co.uk/dsa** or by calling our expert publications team on **0870 850 6553**. The team can give you advice about learning materials and how to prepare for the tests and beyond. They can also help you select a suitable learning material if you have a special need; for example, if you have a learning disability or English isn't your first language.

DSA publications are also available from book shops and online retailers. DSA apps can be downloaded from the iPhone app store and eBooks are available from your device's eBook store.

11

# What is CBT?

Compulsory basic training (CBT) is the course that all learner motorcycle and moped riders must complete before riding on the road.

In addition, holders of a full car licence obtained by passing their driving test on or after 1 February 2001 must complete a CBT course if they wish to validate the full moped entitlement on their driving licence.

CBT can only be given by approved training bodies (ATBs) that have trainers who have been assessed by DSA and sites approved by DSA for off-road training.

CBT allows you to learn the following in a safe environment

- motorcycling theory
- skills that make you safe on the road
- the correct attitude towards motorcycling.

## Exemption from CBT

You don't have to take CBT if you hold a

- full moped licence obtained by passing a moped test after 1 December 1990
- full motorcycle licence for one category and wish to upgrade to another.

You'll also be exempt if you live and ride on specified offshore islands. However, if you ride across to mainland UK you'll need to complete a CBT.

## Certificate of Completion

When you complete a CBT course you'll be given a Certificate of Completion of an Approved Training Course (DL196).

Since 1 February 2001 the DL196 has recorded whether CBT was completed on

- a moped or motorcycle
- a motorcycle/sidecar combination or moped that has more than two wheels.

This will validate your entitlement accordingly.

**Certificate life** CBT certificates have a two-year life.

A certificate validating full moped entitlement on a full car licence will remain valid for mopeds for the life of the licence.

**Motorcycle validation** If training is completed on a motorcycle/sidecar combination or on a moped that has more than two wheels

- moped validation will be limited to mopeds with more than two wheels
- motorcycle validation will be limited to motorcycle/sidecar combinations.

Please note that, from 19 January 2013, tests for mopeds with three or four wheels, 'A1' tricycles, 'A' tricycles and motorcycles with sidecars will only be offered to the physically disabled. See table on pages 20–21 for information or visit **www.gov.uk**

# The CBT course

CBT is arranged so that you progress through a series of elements. You'll only move onto the next element when your trainer is satisfied that you've learnt the necessary theory and demonstrated the practical skills to a safe basic level.

## What are the elements?

Element A – Introduction to CBT

Element B – Practical on-site training

Element C – Practical on-site riding

Element D – Practical on-road training

Element E – Practical on-road riding

The elements must be taken in this order. Each element is described in detail in section 2 (see page 24).

*Your trainer will ensure you complete each element before you progress to the next.*

Within each element the trainer is free to deliver the training in the order which is felt to be most appropriate for you.

The CBT record on page 67 of this book will allow you to record when each of the elements has been completed.

For more information about CBT, visit **youtube.com/watch?v=hOyAWwAWUy4**

## Trainer to trainee ratios

During your CBT you may be accompanied by other learners up to a maximum ratio of

- 4:1 during on-site elements
- 2:1 during the on-road element.

For those using the direct access scheme (see page 18), the ratios are 2:1 for both on-road and off-road elements.

# Approved training bodies

## Types of trainer

CBT can only be given by ATBs using trainers who are either

- DSA-assessed certified trainers or
- down-trained certified trainers.

**DSA-assessed certified trainers** Every ATB must employ at least one trainer who has successfully attended DSA's CBT assessment. They're called Cardington-assessed trainers and can

- provide CBT training and issue DL196 certificates
- down-train other trainers within the ATB.

**Down-trained certified trainers** These trainers have been down-trained by the Cardington-assessed trainer and are qualified to provide CBT training including issuing the DL196 certificate at the end of the course.

**Direct access** Some trainers may have a further qualification allowing them to give direct access instruction. This is obtained by attending DSA's direct access scheme assessment.

**How can I tell which type of trainer is giving me training?** When training, your trainer will be carrying a certificate. If it contains a 'C', they're a Cardington-assessed trainer while a 'D' indicates they're direct access qualified. Some certificates contain both qualifications.

## Quality control

DSA monitors the standard of training given by trainers. If a DSA examiner is present during your training, don't worry. The examiner won't take part in the training; they're only there to safeguard the quality of training you receive.

## Choosing an ATB

You can find out about the ATBs in your area from

- the local road safety officer
- most motorcycle dealers
- motorcycle papers and magazines
- local papers or Yellow Pages
- going online at **www.gov.uk**
- calling DSA on **0300 200 1122**.

## Clothing

Your trainer will discuss motorcycle clothing in detail as part of the CBT course.

If you're just starting to ride, it will pay you to listen to your trainer before rushing out to buy anything.

During your CBT course, you

- must wear the visibility aid provided by the ATB. This will carry the name of the training organisation
- should wear appropriate clothing and stout footwear.

Many ATBs provide basic equipment for the CBT course (see Element A page 25).

*Use your trainer's experience to make sure you get the best clothing you can for your money.*

## Hiring a motorcycle

ATBs usually have motorcycles you can hire for your CBT, practical test or additional training.

These may be learner-rated motorcycles or direct access-rated motorcycles. Talk to local ATBs to find out what they can offer.

If you hire equipment and the machine from the ATB, they should provide the necessary insurance.

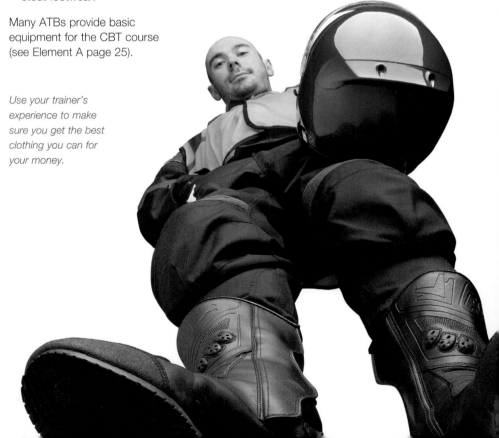

# Your motorcycle licence

To begin riding a motorcycle on the road you must

- be at least 17 years old
- hold a valid DL196 certificate
- hold a driving licence which allows you to ride motorcycles (category A).

That licence can be either of the following

- a provisional driving licence. This provides provisional car, motorcycle and moped entitlement
- a full car or moped licence. This provides provisional motorcycle entitlement.

All riders **MUST** wear a safety helmet at all times when riding (unless they're a member of the Sikh religion and wear a turban) and ensure any helmet visor used conforms to BSI standards (see page 27).

For a list of motorcycles that can be used for practical tests, visit **dft.gov.uk/motorcycle-test-vehicle-list**

## Provisional motorcycle entitlement

After completing CBT, learners may ride a solo motorcycle up to 125 cc or with a power output of no more than 11 kW.

With provisional motorcycle entitlement you **MUST NOT**

- ride on motorways
- carry a pillion passenger
- ride without red L plates fitted to both front and rear of the motorcycle (in Wales you may display red D plates). If you cross from Wales into another part of the UK you **MUST** display red L plates.

### Does a non-UK driving licence entitle me to ride?

You can ride for one year from the date of entry to the UK if you hold a valid foreign licence. After this you may be required to take a test depending on the country of origin of your licence. For further information please contact DVLA on **0300 790 6801**.

### Do I need to request motorcycle entitlement to be added?

Since March 2002 provisional motorcycle entitlement has automatically been included on driving licences. If you hold a provisional licence where the motorcycle entitlement has expired you'll need to contact DVLA for a replacement licence. See pages 20–21 for more information or visit **www.gov.uk**

**What are the rules concerning test motorcycles?**

Motorcycles less than 120 cc aren't acceptable for the practical motorcycle test.

Only the disabled can use a trike or a motorcycle/sidecar combination for the test. (See notes below table on page 21.)

The licence obtained will be restricted to such combinations.

If you pass your test on a motorcycle with automatic or semi-automatic transmission this will be recorded on your licence. Your full licence entitlement will be restricted to motorcycles in this category.

## Full motorcycle licence

From 19 January 2013, there will be three categories of motorcycle licence: categories A, A1 and A2. The table below explains what you can ride and at what age.

| Category | Description | Minimum age |
|---|---|---|
| A1 | A motorcycle with a cylinder capacity not exceeding 125 cc, of a power not exceeding 11 kW (14.6 bhp) and with a power-to-weight ratio not exceeding 0.1 kW per kg | 17 |
| | A motor tricycle with power not exceeding 15 kW | 17 |
| A2 | A motorcycle of a power not exceeding 35 kW (46.6 bhp), with a power-to-weight ratio not exceeding 0.2 kW per kg and not being derived from a vehicle of more than double its power | 19 |
| A | Any motorcycle of a power exceeding 35 kW (46.6 bhp) or with a power-to-weight ratio exceeding 0.2 kW per kg | 24* |
| | A motor tricycle with a power exceeding 15 kW | 24 |

* Age 21 if you have two years' experience on an A2 motorcycle and you pass a further practical test

## Progressive access

Riders who wish to progress from category A1 to A2 or from A2 to A must pass a practical test to obtain each licence category. This test will only be available when the licence for the lower category has been held for at least two years.

## Obtaining a motorcycle licence

### Category A1

A full A1 licence allows you to ride motorcycles with an engine not exceeding 125 cc and with a power output of up to 11 kW (14.6 bhp). To obtain a category A1 licence, you must

- be at least 17 years old

- successfully complete a CBT course

- pass the motorcycle theory test

- pass the practical motorcycle test on a motorcycle

  – with a cubic capacity of between 120 cc and 125 cc

  – with an engine power output of up to 11 kW (14.6 bhp)

  – capable of a speed of at least 90 km/h (55 mph).

## Category A2

A full A2 licence allows you to ride machines with a power output of up to 35 kW (46.6 bhp). To obtain a category A2 licence you must

- be at least 19 years old
- successfully complete a CBT course
- pass the motorcycle theory test
- pass the practical motorcycle test on a motorcycle
  - with a cubic capacity of at least 395 cc
  - with an engine power of between 25 kW* and 35 kW (33 bhp* to 46.6 bhp) (*drops to 20 kW/27 bhp from 31 December 2013 onwards)
  - with a power-to-weight ratio not exceeding 0.2 kW/kg
  - that, if restricted, isn't derived from a machine more than double its power.

Alternatively, you can take a category A2 practical test under progressive access. If you already have an A1 licence that you've held for a minimum of two years you don't need to

- take another theory test
- hold a CBT certificate.

## Category A

A full category A licence gives you full entitlement to all motorcycles. You can obtain a category A licence either under progressive access, or, at age 24 and over, under the direct access scheme.

### Category A under progressive access

Under progressive access you can take a category A practical test at age 21 if you already have an A2 licence that you've held for a minimum of two years. You don't need to

- take another theory test
- hold a CBT certificate.

---

### Will I have to take a theory test?

All candidates for a practical test must first pass a motorcycle theory test, unless upgrading from A1 to A2 or A2 to A under the progressive access route.

Note: If you're upgrading for any other reason, you'll need to hold a valid theory test certificate.

### What defines a moped?

A moped must have an engine capacity under 50 cc and not weigh more than 250 kg.

If it was registered after 1 August 1977, its maximum design speed can't exceed 50 km/h (about 32 mph). Mopeds built after June 2003 are restricted to 45 km/h (28 mph).

### Category A under direct access

This is for riders aged 24 and over. To obtain a category A licence you must

- successfully complete a CBT course
- pass the motorcycle theory test
- pass the practical motorcycle test.

Passing the practical test on a motorcycle of at least 40 kW (53.6 bhp) gives immediate access to all sizes of motorcycle.

Under direct access you can practise on any size of motorcycle that exceeds the UK learner specification provided that

- you're accompanied at all times by a qualified approved trainer, who is on another motorcycle and in radio contact with you
- fluorescent or reflective safety clothing is worn during supervision
- red L plates (D plates in Wales) are fitted and provisional licence restrictions followed.

For more information about the new rules for riding a motorcycle or moped, visit **youtube.com/watch?v=CVZP0VzIj_4**

## Full licence entitlement

With a full motorcycle licence you may

- ride without L plates (or D plates in Wales)
- carry a pillion passenger
- use motorways.

## Routes to motorcycle licences

| Old licence category | New licence category | Minimum test vehicles EU requirements from 19 January 2013 | Min age limit | Access requirements |
|---|---|---|---|---|
| P | AM mopeds | Two-wheeled machine with a cubic capacity of no more than 50 cc and a maximum design speed not exceeding 45 km/h (28 mph). **DSA proposes to accept all 'learner legal' machines for test unless there's clear evidence they don't meet the new requirements.** | 16 | CBT, theory and practical tests |
| A1 | A1 | Motorcycle without sidecar, with a cubic capacity of at least 120 cc, no more than 125 cc, and a power output not exceeding 11 kW (14.6 bhp), capable of a speed of at least 90 km/h (55 mph). | 17 | CBT, theory and practical tests |
|  | A2 | Motorcycle without sidecar, with a cubic capacity of at least 395 cc and an engine power of at least 25 kW** (33 bhp**) not exceeding 35 kW (46.6 bhp) with a power-to-weight ratio not exceeding 0.2 kW/kg not derived from a vehicle more than double its power. | 19 | **(Progressive access)** Held A1 licence for a minimum of 2 years – take either a practical test **OR** Hold a valid CBT and theory test certificate and take practical test. |
| A | A | Motorcycle without a sidecar with a cubic capacity of at least 595 cc and an engine power of at least 40 kW – 53.6 bhp. | 21 | **(Progressive access)** Held A2 licence for a minimum of 2 years – take a practical test |
|  |  |  | 24 | **(Direct access)** Hold a valid CBT and theory test certificate and take a practical test. |

\*    Restricted motorcycles – Any switchable or variable restriction device must be installed by a reliable source and certified with documentary evidence from a main dealer, an official importer or a recognised specialist in restricting vehicles. It must be clearly evident to the examiner which power mode it is set to. An engine control unit (ECU) or power controller that has a clearly visible, switchable power setting would be acceptable for test. Interchangeable carburettor heads/exhaust manifold restrictor or a hidden ECU would not be acceptable for multi-category testing. Any machine which is being used for multiple categories (A2 and A) must be easily recognisable as to which category it is presented for. Evidence of restriction should be in the form of a certificate or on headed paper from an official source such as a main dealer, official importer or recognised specialist in restricting vehicles and must show the vehicle registration number. You'll only need to show the certificate once unless you're using the vehicle at more than one test centre. You're advised to store a copy on the bike, for example under the saddle.

\*\*   Drops to 20 kW/27 bhp from 31 December 2013 onwards.

## Other rider information

**New riders from 19 Jan 2013 onwards** – Moped entitlement will show on licence as 'AM, Q'. See access requirements. If you pass your car test first, you will have the moped entitlement but will have to pass CBT to ride one on the road.

**Existing riders with entitlement gained before 19 Jan 2013** – If you already have moped entitlement, you will keep it (engine size up to 50 cc and max speed up to 50 km/h). On new/replacement licences issued to you, this will show as categories AM, P and Q. To retain your existing entitlement, P extends the AM category to include two- or three-wheeled mopeds with a higher speed of up to 50 km/h and Q extends the AM category to include two- or three-wheeled mopeds with a speed of up to 25 km/h. If you already have motorcycle entitlement it won't change under the new rules. However, if you want to ride bigger motorcycles, you'll need to follow the rules for new riders. Your entitlement to ride tricycles is currently shown on your licence as category B1 (tricycles and quads) or B (cars). When you replace or renew your licence after 19 January 2013, it will be shown as B1 and A (limited to tricycles).

### This licence category covers small motorcycles up to 11 kW and 125 cc, and motor tricycles with a power output not more than 15 kW.

**DSA proposes to accept all 'learner legal' machines for test unless there's clear evidence they don't meet the new requirements.**
A three-wheeled moped or motorcycle is only suitable for test if the distance measured between the centre of the area of contact with the road surface of the two wheels is less than 460 millimetres (46 cm).

### This licence category covers medium motorcycles up to 35 kW.

**DSA will accept**
- **evidence from manufacturers or official importers that a specific model of motorcycle meets these requirements**
- **an individual machine that has been restricted to comply for test as long as you show certified proof of restriction to the examiner. A dyno test certificate is not acceptable.**

When wishing to move up to bigger motorcycles, remember that you will be classed as a learner on the larger machine and **MUST NOT** ride it on motorways until you have passed the appropriate test in that category.

### This licence category covers motorcycles of unlimited size and power, with or without sidecar, and motor tricycles with a power output of more than 15 kW.

**DSA will accept evidence from manufacturers or official importers that a specific model of motorcycle meets these requirements and will publish this information where it applies to a number of machines of a specific type. Dyno certificates are not acceptable.**
When wishing to move up to bigger motorcycles, remember that you will be classed as a learner on the larger machine and **MUST NOT** ride it on motorways until you have passed the appropriate test in that category.

A valid theory test certificate is always required before taking the first practical motorcycle test and, unless taking the progressive access route, a valid theory test certificate is required before taking any subsequent practical motorcycle tests.

Tricycles – You'll need to follow the same rules if you want to ride a tricycle that falls within these categories. PLEASE NOTE that tests for mopeds with three or four wheels (see exception above), A1 tricycles, A tricycles and motorcycles with sidecars will only be offered to the physically disabled.

All categories – Additional machines can be added to the list of those known to comply if there's enough evidence that they meet the new rules; this should be either a certificate or on headed paper from an official source such as the manufacturer, a main dealer or an official importer. The candidate is responsible for making sure the machine meets the new rules; if their machine doesn't comply, their test may be cancelled and they may lose their test fee. Different arrangements apply to candidates with a physical disability.

For information and further updates, see **assets.dft.gov.uk/dsa/dsa-routes-to-your-motorcycle-licence.pdf** or visit **www.gov.uk**

## Moped riders

To ride a moped on the road you must be at least 16 years old and have a driving licence that entitles you to ride mopeds. Category P is the national category; AM is the new European category from 19 January 2013 (see table on pages 20–21). At 16 years old this can be a full or provisional moped licence.

For 17 and over it can also be a

- full car licence (see right)
- full motorcycle licence
- provisional driving licence. This provides provisional moped entitlement.

**Remember,** the same DL196 that validates your full moped entitlement will have a limited life (see Certificate life on page 12) for validating provisional motorcycle entitlement.

**Provisional moped entitlement**  After completing CBT this allows you to ride a moped. You **MUST NOT** carry a pillion passenger, ride on motorways or ride without red L plates (or D plates in Wales) fitted to both the front and the rear.

**Full moped licence**  Full moped entitlement allows you to ride mopeds without red L plates and carry a pillion passenger.

Mopeds aren't allowed on motorways, even if you hold a full licence.

## Full car licence holders

Holders of a full car licence obtained by passing their driving test before 1 February 2001 hold unconditional full moped entitlement.

Holders of a full car licence obtained by passing their driving test on or after 1 February 2001, who don't already hold a full moped or motorcycle licence, **MUST** hold a valid CBT completion certificate (DL196) to validate their full moped entitlement.

If a valid DL196 is already held when the car test is passed, the full moped entitlement will be validated immediately.

A DL196 validating full moped entitlement on a full car licence will remain valid for mopeds for the life of the licence. It's therefore particularly important that the DL196 is kept safe.

# section **two**
# COMPULSORY BASIC TRAINING

This section covers

- Element A – Introduction to CBT
- Element B – Practical on-site training
- Element C – Practical on-site riding
- Element D – Practical on-road training
- Element E – Practical on-road riding
- CBT record
- After CBT

# Element A
# **Introduction to CBT**

This element is an introduction to CBT. It will take the form of a discussion. Your trainer will explain the basics and not get involved in complicated issues.

Wherever possible your trainer will use examples to help demonstrate the point being made.

As a part of this element you'll have your entitlement to ride motorcycles checked.

If necessary your trainer will explain what you need to do in order to obtain this entitlement.

At the end of this module you should understand the purpose and content of CBT. Many experienced car drivers who take up motorcycling find that CBT is an eye-opening experience which increases their awareness of hazards.

*Your trainer will progress through the course at a pace that suits you. Don't be afraid to ask if you haven't understood something.*

## CBT overview

You can't ride on the road until you've satisfactorily completed all the elements of CBT. Your trainer will explain the aims of CBT and will also explain why it was introduced. An overview of the course content should be given.

**Remember,** don't treat CBT as a formality you must grudgingly endure. Trainers are experienced motorcyclists who have valuable advice to give learner riders and are motorcycle enthusiasts.

Take the CBT course seriously and enjoy learning safely.

The time it takes to complete the course will be determined by you. Your trainer shouldn't move you on to the next part until you're ready.

Within each element, trainers are free to deliver the topics in the order that they find best for you. Every topic must, however, be covered to the necessary level.

You'll need to demonstrate to your trainer that you have a basic skill level and an understanding of each topic. This may be through question and answer sessions for the theory or through practical demonstrations of your riding ability.

## Equipment and clothing

Your trainer will explain the different types of motorcycle clothing available. As well as looking at outer clothing, the talk will include helmets, visors and goggles, gloves and boots.

Motorcycle clothing is generally expensive and your trainer will help prioritise what you should buy first and identify less expensive alternatives. You should also discuss the effects of getting cold and wet and how some clothing can help protect from certain injuries.

*As well as being a good fit, your helmet must be correctly fastened.*

> **Remember,** you must also know the dangers of riding
>
> • with scratched, damaged and tinted visors or goggles (or without eye protection)
> • with a damaged helmet
> • without gloves or in inappropriate clothing
> • without adequate clothing in bad weather.

**Safety helmets** By law, you **MUST** wear a safety helmet when riding a motorcycle on the road (members of the Sikh religion who wear a turban are exempt). All helmets sold in the UK **MUST**

• comply with British Standard BS 6658:1985 and carry the BSI kitemark

• comply with UNECE Regulation 22.05 (it will be marked with a UN 'E' mark – the first two digits of the approval number will be '05') or

• comply with any standard accepted by a member of the European Economic Area (EEA) state which offers a level of safety and protection equivalent to BS 6658:1985 and carry a mark equivalent to the BSI kitemark.

For the latest helmet safety standards, visit **www.gov.uk**

**Visors and goggles** A visor or goggles are vital to protect your eyes from wind, rain, insects and road dirt. All visors and goggles **MUST**

• comply with British Standard BS 4110 Grade X, XA, YA or ZA

• display a BSI kitemark or

• comply with a European standard which offers a level of safety and protection at least equivalent to these British Standards and carry a mark equivalent to the BSI kitemark (ECE 22-05).

Goggles may comply with the EU Directive on Personal Protective Equipment and carry the 'CE' mark.

## Eyesight check

At this stage in CBT your trainer will check your eyesight. The regulations state that, in good daylight, you **MUST** be able to read a vehicle number plate with letters 79.4 mm (3.1 inches) high at a minimum distance of 20 metres (about 66 feet). These are the number plates in the format XX50XXX.

Number plates in the older format (for example X123XXX) have a wider font and should be read from a distance of 20.5 metres (about 67 feet).

*Your trainer will check your eyesight by asking you to read a number plate from a set distance.*

### What if I can't read the number plate?

If you can't read the number plate at the minimum distance your course can't continue. You must demonstrate that your eyesight meets the legal minimum requirements using glasses or contact lenses if necessary, before further elements can be taken.

If you use glasses or contact lenses to enable you to read the number plate, you must wear them for the rest of the course and whenever you ride on the road.

### What safety issues will I need to know about?

You'll need to understand the legal requirements for helmets and how to fasten your helmet securely. You also need to know about the BSI kitemark on visors and goggles.

### How do I stop my visor from steaming up?

There are anti-fog visors available which can help reduce fogging but if you already have a standard visor you could use an anti-fog spray.

# Element B
# Practical on-site training

This element provides you with an introduction to the motorcycle. You won't start riding the motorcycle in this element although you'll get hands-on training.

At the end of this element you'll be able to show a working knowledge of the machine and should have a feel for the weight and balance of a motorcycle.

## Motorcycle controls

Your trainer will explain the controls in a logical order. The controls covered include

- **hand controls** throttle, front brake, clutch, indicators, choke, electric starter, engine cut-off or kill switch, lighting switches, horn, fuel tap

- **foot controls** rear brake, kick starter, gear change lever

- **instruments** speedometer, rev counter, warning lamps, water temperature and fuel gauges.

**Basic skills** Practise finding and using the controls. Some controls are adjustable. Your trainer will explain how they can be set up to suit you.

You'll also need to develop a feel for the controls.

It shouldn't require great strength or force to operate the motorcycle's controls. Be especially careful with the throttle, clutch and brakes.

**Remember,** that when riding you'll be wearing gloves and boots. This may affect the feel and ease with which you can reach certain controls.

You must be able to operate the controls smoothly and without having to look down to find them.

## Basic safety checks and use of the stands

Your trainer will show you how to make basic checks to ensure your motorcycle is safe. These checks will include the

- brakes – correct operation and adjustment
- steering head – wear and adjustment
- control cables – wear, adjustment and lubrication
- fluid levels – hydraulic brake fluid, engine oil, coolant, battery electrolyte
- lights
- suspension
- wheels and spokes
- tyres – wear, damage and pressure
- drive chain – wear, lubrication and tension
- nuts and bolts for tightness
- number plate and reflectors for visibility
- mirrors for clarity.

You'll also be shown the types of motorcycle stands and how and when to use them.

**Basic skills** While you're not expected to become a motorcycle mechanic, you'll need to be able to recognise basic faults that could affect your motorcycle's roadworthiness.

When using the stands you need to

- demonstrate the correct techniques for putting a motorcycle onto and off its stands
- show an understanding of the effects of camber and gradient.

It's important that you know which machine checks you need to make on a daily basis and which can be left longer.

Make sure you can manage to use the stands correctly. Incorrect methods of using the stands can lead to personal injury or damage to the machine.

## Wheeling the motorcycle and braking to stop

You'll learn how to balance a motorcycle while wheeling it both to the left and right (in either order).

Your trainer will show you

- where to stand
- how to hold the motorcycle
- how to lean the motorcycle.

In addition you'll be taught how to use the front brake to stop in a controlled manner. This will involve

- making sure the motorcycle is upright
- practice to get the feel of the front brake.

**Basic skills** You'll have to demonstrate

- full control of the motorcycle while wheeling it
- that you have the necessary balance skills.

Your trainer will want to see that you can squeeze the front brake gently and effectively to stop.

When wheeling the motorcycle, avoid

- holding somewhere other than the handlebar grips
- wobbling
- insecure control
- looking down
- harsh use of the front brake.

## Starting and stopping the engine

Your trainer will show you what checks you need to make before starting the engine. A mnemonic such as FIGS may be used (see box opposite).

**Basic skills** Before starting the engine you'll need to

- be able to find neutral and recognise a 'false neutral'
- demonstrate that you know how to operate the ignition switch and any immobiliser fitted
- know how to operate the starter mechanism fitted to your machine.

Before you start the engine don't forget to turn on the fuel. The engine may well start but will splutter and cut out before you've travelled far if you don't.

Only use the choke for the shortest period necessary. Running with the choke on for longer than you need to can cause

- the engine to run too fast when you're trying to slow down
- increased wear on the engine
- more fuel to be used and more pollution produced.

When starting the engine

- make sure you've selected neutral
- don't hold the kick start lever down after the kick-over
- don't hold the starter button on after the engine has started.

When stopping the engine don't

- use the kill switch unless in an emergency
- forget to switch off the fuel tap (if fitted).

*Many motorcycles have a rev counter that shows how fast the engine is running.*

Fuel

Ignition

Gears

Start

## What does FIGS stand for?

**Fuel** The use of the choke will be explained and you'll be shown how to

- check for fuel in the tank
- turn on the fuel tap
- use the reserve position.

**Ignition** The engine kill switch will be explained and you'll be shown

- the positions on the ignition switch
- how to switch on the ignition.

**Gears** Checking for neutral by

- checking the neutral lamp
- rocking the machine back and forward
- spinning the rear wheel on the stand.

**Start** You should be shown how to use

- electric starters
- kick starters.

It's important that you know how to operate a kick start but most modern bikes will have electronic starters.

# Element C
# **Practical on-site riding**

In this element you'll begin riding a motorcycle. By the time you've finished this element you'll have developed enough basic skills to allow you to ride a motorcycle under control.

You'll learn the essential techniques including rear observation and the Observation – Signal – Manoeuvre (OSM) and Position – Speed – Look (PSL) routines.

You'll practise these practical skills until your trainer is satisfied that you'll be safe when you're taken out onto the road.

## Riding in a straight line and stopping

This is the point in CBT where you begin riding a motorcycle. Your trainer will explain and may also demonstrate what's required. You'll be shown how to move off and how to stop. This will include

- using the clutch
- selecting first gear
- finding the 'biting point'
- keeping balance
- using the brakes to stop.

Covering the rear brake will be explained to you and you'll be expected to put this into practice. Your trainer will also show you how to ride in a straight line, including advice on how to keep your balance.

**Basic skills** You'll need to practise until you can

- keep your balance
- coordinate the controls when moving off and stopping

- use both brakes in a smooth and controlled manner.

**Try to avoid**

- riding with your feet hanging down
- looking down instead of ahead while riding.

When you move off for the first time you may feel insecure. However, from the beginning, learn to ride with your feet up on the footrests and watch the road ahead.

When you stop you'll have to put a foot down to support the motorcycle. Your trainer will explain which foot to put down. Follow the guidance and make sure you understand why.

Avoid fierce use of the controls at all times as this can lead to stalling the engine, skidding or loss of steering control.

## Riding slowly

You'll have to show you can ride a motorcycle slowly and under full control.

This is to prepare you for riding on the road where this skill will be needed to deal with

- junctions
- slow-moving traffic in queues
- hazards.

A demonstration of what's required will probably be given to help show the level of control achievable and how slowly you'll be expected to ride.

**Basic skills** You'll need to keep your balance and steering under control while riding slowly.

### Try to avoid

- loss of balance
- loss of steering control
- harsh use of throttle and brakes
- riding too fast
- not using the footrests.

*Use all of your fingers on the front brake lever for maximum control and stopping power.*

*To begin with you may find it difficult to feel how hard you're pressing the rear brake.*

## Using the brakes

You need to be able to operate the brakes in a controlled manner so that you can

- control your speed
- stop accurately.

You'll be shown how to use both brakes together for maximum control and stopping ability.

The importance of this skill can be related to the need to stop accurately at junctions.

**Basic skills** Your trainer will expect you to stop the motorcycle at a marked position. Cones, a line or some other marker may be used to identify where you're expected to stop.

**Try to avoid**

- stalling as you stop
- use of the rear brake before the front
- use of one brake only
- harsh and late use of the brakes
- locking the wheels
- inaccurate stopping.

### What if I brake too hard?

If you brake too hard the affected wheel will lock-up and skid. If this happens you need to release the brake momentarily and then reapply it as firmly as the conditions permit.

### What are linked brakes?

Linked braking systems are where the use of one brake control activates both brakes. For maximum braking you'll still need to make proper use of both brakes together.

## Changing gear

You need to be able to change up and down smoothly through the gears.

Your trainer will explain how to operate the controls to achieve smooth gear changes. The space on the training area may limit practice to second or third gear.

### Try to avoid

- harsh use of the controls
- failing to coordinate clutch, throttle and gear change lever
- selecting the wrong gear.

**Basic skills** You'll need to demonstrate that you can

- coordinate the controls
- make upward and downward gear changes satisfactorily.

## Riding a figure of eight

This exercise is to develop steering and balance control when changing from one lock to another.

There are no set size measurements for this exercise. Your trainer may start off with a large layout and reduce it as your skill develops.

**Basic skills** You'll learn slow speed steering and balance control.

### Try to avoid

- riding with your feet off the footrests
- harsh throttle and clutch control
- excessive speed
- wobbling.

*Riding a figure of eight around cones will help develop your control, steering and balance while travelling at low speeds.*

*Riding in a figure of eight gives you the chance to practise turning to both left and right at slow speeds in one manoeuvre.*

## Emergency stop

You must be able to stop safely should an emergency arise. Your trainer will explain the effects of applying the brakes individually and using them together.

This may then be followed by a demonstration to highlight the points.

You need to understand

• how weight is transferred during heavy braking

• how weight transfer can affect the rear wheel.

Reference may be made to using the brakes in the ratio 75% front and 25% rear on a dry road surface and 50% front and 50% rear on a wet road surface. It's important to understand that this refers to braking force, not lever movement.

**Basic skills** You must be able to coordinate front and rear brakes correctly and in the correct ratio for the conditions, as well as being able to avoid skidding.

**Try to avoid**

• late reactions when signalled to stop

• excessive brake pressure causing either or both wheels to lock

• not responding to the weather and road conditions

• not using the clutch as you stop.

41

## Rear observation

To be safe on the road you should know as much about the traffic behind as you can.

On a motorcycle you can find out about traffic behind by

- using the mirrors
- turning and looking over your shoulder.

Your trainer will explain the special requirements for a motorcyclist including

- how and when to use mirrors
- how to overcome the blind spots.

You should practise looking round before moving off and while on the move.

**Basic skills** You'll need to practise using your mirrors and looking around while moving so that you can

- see what's behind you
- check blind spots
- keep control while looking around.

**Try to avoid**

- looking round for an excessive time
- veering off-course while looking round
- poorly timed rearward glances.

Left-hand mirror vision

Forward vision

Right-hand mirror vision

# Turning left and right

You need to be able to deal safely with road junctions. Your trainer will explain the OSM (Observation – Signal – Manoeuvre) and PSL (Position – Speed – Look) routines and may give a demonstration.

Use of the mirrors and the 'lifesaver' look will be explained.

An explanation of different junction types, road markings and traffic signals and signs will also be given.

You'll need to know how to deal with left and right turns, minor to major and major to minor. A mock junction layout may be set out on the training area for practice.

**Basic skills** Right and left turns require different procedures. You need to

• recognise the different types of turn
• demonstrate correct road positioning
• make effective observation
• give correct signals in good time.

**Try to avoid**

• making badly timed rearward or sideways glances
• giving badly timed or incorrect signals
• looking around when the situation calls for concentration ahead
• not cancelling signals after turning.

*The skills you gain in this exercise will be needed in both Element E and during the practical motorcycle test.*

## U-turn

Riding a U-turn is a set exercise which also has practical use when riding on the road.

You need to be able to ride your motorcycle around in a U-turn

- under control
- with your feet on the footrests
- keeping aware of the traffic conditions.

Your trainer may demonstrate the level of balance, steering and control needed for this exercise.

You'll be given the chance to practise until you're confident of your ability.

**Basic skills** To ride around in a U-turn you need to be able to coordinate and control your

- balance
- steering
- use of the clutch, throttle and rear brake.

In addition you need to understand when, how and where to look for traffic or other hazards.

**Try to avoid**

- harsh use of the controls
- not taking effective observation
- using your feet to help overcome poor balance.

# Element D
## Practical on-road training

Having carried out theory and practical training off-road, your trainer will now prepare you for the on-road element of CBT. The knowledge you gain now will be the foundations on which to build your motorcycling career.

This element will cover the information you need to ride legally and safely on the road.

During Element E aspects of this theory may be reinforced in practical situations.

*Being small, a motorcycle can be difficult to see, especially at some road junctions.*

*At night, reflective materials help you to be seen because they shine brightly in the beam of other vehicles' headlights.*

## Conspicuity

It's vitally important to understand why you need to be conspicuous when riding a motorcycle.

Your trainer will discuss why you may not be seen and how you can make it easier for others to see you. The talk will include

- visibility aids
- differences between fluorescent materials and reflective materials
- use of headlights
- road positioning
- clothing
- keeping your motorcycle clean.

This may be illustrated by a short video presentation.

In addition, there will be some discussion on the legal requirements to use dipped headlights in poor visibility.

Making yourself conspicuous isn't a legal requirement. However, it's in your own interest to make yourself easier to see. To do so, avoid

- wearing dull clothing
- riding a dirty motorcycle
- riding in another road user's blind area.

## Legal requirements

Before you ride on the road there are minimum legal requirements of which you **MUST** be aware.

Your trainer will explain about

• road tax, insurance and MOT certificates

• provisional motorcycle licence entitlement

• DL196 (CBT completion certificate)

• L plates.

In addition you need to know about general roadworthiness and the legal requirement to fasten your helmet correctly.

Make sure you have all the legal aspects in order before riding on the road. You'll not always be sent a reminder when certain mandatory items need renewal or expire such as

• MOT certificates

• DL196 certificates.

Don't get caught out through neglecting to keep everything up to date.

*Routine checks on your motorcycle are necessary to keep it roadworthy.*

## Vulnerability

As a motorcyclist you're generally more vulnerable than other motorists. Your trainer will explain about the dangers of

- falling off
- collision, even at low speed
- weather conditions
- road surface conditions.

The head and limbs are the most exposed parts of your body when riding. Your trainer will tell you what steps you can take to protect yourself from injury and the effects of the weather.

Always buy the best protective equipment you can afford, but don't

- use a helmet that's damaged, second-hand, fits poorly or is unfastened
- ride without protective clothing
- ride too fast for the conditions.

## Speed

You need to understand why riding at the correct speed is so important. Riding too slowly can be just as much a problem as riding too fast.

**Remember,** you need to develop a defensive riding style so that you can always stop

- within your range of vision
- in case a potential hazard turns into a real danger.

Your trainer will explain about the

- legal speed limits
- suitable use of speed
- consequences of speeding and riding too slowly.

Always ride within speed limits and your ability.

*It's essential that you keep up to date, make sure you have a copy of The Highway Code.*

*Anticipating the actions of other road users is a vital part of defensive riding.*

## The Highway Code

As a road user you should own a current copy of The Highway Code and refer to it often. Without knowledge of The Highway Code, you'll find it difficult to deal with all aspects of training.

While The Highway Code contains all the essential elements of road safety, specific elements relating to CBT will be covered in more detail by your trainer.

Don't treat The Highway Code as a book to learn just for your tests. It contains a wealth of legislative instruction, other information and general advice which is designed to keep you safe and legal whenever you use the road.

Refer to it often and follow the advice and legal instructions it contains.

## Anticipation

At all times you should ride defensively and anticipate the actions of other road users.

Your trainer will explain that to anticipate you need to

- look well ahead
- plan ahead
- develop hazard awareness
- concentrate at all times.

**Remember,** anticipation is a skill that develops over time. Signs that show a lack of anticipation include late and harsh braking, being distracted and not taking road and weather conditions into account.

During discussion your trainer will cover a variety of scenarios which illustrate the point being made.

## Rear observation

You must understand that rear observation is a combination of using the mirrors and looking around.

Your trainer will explain about

- effective rear observation
- timing of rearward glances
- 'lifesaver' checks.

Some time may be spent discussing the effects of looking around at the wrong moment.

Take care not to

- veer off-course while looking round
- look around too late
- look around when you should be concentrating ahead.

*Correctly timed rearward glances are an important part of safe riding. But, remember, don't lose track of what's developing in front.*

*When passing parked vehicles you need to think about hazards such as doors suddenly opening or oncoming traffic. Take up the correct position so that you can deal with these hazards safely.*

## Road positioning

It's important that you understand where you should position yourself when riding on the road.

Points which will be covered include how you should position yourself to deal with

- bends
- junctions
- road conditions
- single and dual carriageways
- hazards
- overtaking.

When you ride on the road always concentrate and avoid

- riding in the gutter
- erratic steering and veering across your lane
- failing to return to your normal position after dealing with a hazard
- riding on the crown of the road as a normal position.

**Remember,** when riding around a right-hand bend don't let yourself cross onto the opposite side of the road as your motorcycle leans.

## Separation distance

You must understand the importance of leaving sufficient space when following another vehicle.

This will involve discussing the advantages of allowing plenty of space such as

• increased ability to see past vehicles ahead and so allow for better forward planning
• increased likelihood of being seen by other road users.

The 'two-second rule' will be explained, and how this is affected by road and weather conditions should also be covered.

The special advice for following large vehicles will also be discussed.

Always keep the correct separation distance from the vehicle ahead and allow for the effect that road and weather conditions have on your stopping distance. If you're too close behind a large vehicle, the driver might not be able to see you in their mirrors.

*Road signs make good markers for using the two-second rule.*

### What are the usual stopping distances?

You should leave enough space between you and the vehicle in front so that you can pull up safely if it suddenly slows or stops.

The safe rule is never to get closer than the overall stopping distances shown below. Don't forget that in wet weather these distances will need to be doubled and can increase up to 10 times in icy conditions.

| Speed | thinking | braking | distance |
|---|---|---|---|
| 20 mph | 6 | 6 | 12 metres or 3 car lengths |
| 30 mph | 9 | 14 | 23 metres or 6 car lengths |
| 40 mph | 12 | 24 | 36 metres or 9 car lengths |
| 50 mph | 15 | 38 | 53 metres or 13 car lengths |
| 60 mph | 18 | 55 | 73 metres or 18 car lengths |
| 70 mph | 21 | 75 | 96 metres or 24 car lengths |

thinking distance

braking distance

Average car length = 4 metres

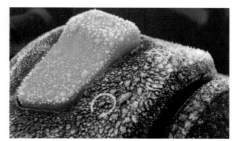

## Weather conditions

Motorcyclists are affected more by weather conditions than most other road users.

You can expect some discussion on how these types of weather conditions affect motorcyclists

- low sun
- wind and rain
- fog
- ice, snow and sleet.

In addition your trainer will explain how these weather conditions affect oil spillage, painted road markings and drain covers.

There should be discussion on turbulence caused by large vehicles and the effect that buffeting can have on motorcyclists.

**Remember,** always respect the effects that weather can have when you're riding a motorcycle.

If in doubt, don't set out!

During your training you're unlikely to encounter severe bad weather conditions. When you do find yourself having to ride in such conditions remember the advice your trainer has given.

## Road surfaces

You need to be aware of how road conditions can affect a motorcyclist.

There are a variety of road surface hazards which will be explained including

- mud and leaves
- gravel and chippings
- tram and railway lines
- studs
- road markings
- potholes or cracks
- drain covers
- shiny surfaces at junctions and roundabouts.

Clues that can help new riders will be discussed, such as

- rainbow colourings on a wet road indicating oil or fuel spillage
- 'loose chippings' road signs
- mud near farm and field entrances.

**Remember,** when you're riding always take the road conditions into account, especially when
- cornering
- accelerating
- braking.

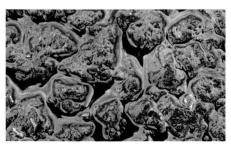

## Alcohol and drugs

**Alcohol** You're required to know that it's a criminal offence to ride with more than the legal level of alcohol in your blood. Your trainer will make it clear that despite legally accepted limits, if you want to be safe and you're going to ride, you shouldn't drink at all.

**The legal limits for riding** Legal riding limits vary across the world. In the UK and Ireland the legal limit is 80 mg/100ml alcohol content in blood. However, it's always advisable **never** to drink and ride. Even at the legal limit you'll have reduced inhibitions.

Be aware that alcohol may remain in the body for around 24–28 hours. Your ability to react quickly may be reduced and the effects will still be evident the next morning, so you could still fail a breath test.

Your body tissues actually need up to 48 hours to recover, although your breath/blood alcohol levels may appear normal after 24 hours. The only safe limit, **ever**, is a zero limit.

**Drugs** Taking certain drugs when you're going to ride is a criminal offence. Many of the effects of drugs will remain in the body for up to 72 hours. Your trainer will cover

- the effect that drugs can have on concentration
- over-the-counter medicines
- how to check whether any medication will affect your riding ability
- how insurance policies could be invalidated.

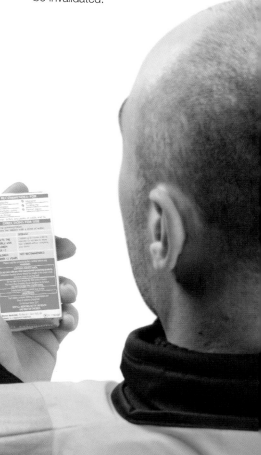

*Medicine manufacturers label their products to help you identify those that could affect your ability to ride safely. If in doubt ask the chemist or your doctor.*

*Some road users will require particular care and early recognition of the hazard is vital if you're going to respond in good time.*

## Attitude

Your trainer will explain how your attitude can affect your safety. The points raised should include the

- effects of riding while angry
- importance of showing patience
- benefits of riding defensively.

Your attitude is under your control. You could put yourself at additional risk by

- riding while upset or angry
- riding in a spirit of competition on the road
- giving offence or provoking reaction by creating dangerous situations.

## Hazard perception

You'll be given some idea of what's meant by a hazard.

> **Remember,** always keep up to date with the constantly changing road and traffic situations by concentrating at all times and looking well ahead.

Your trainer will explain

- the importance of planning ahead
- how early recognition makes hazards easier to deal with
- the need for concentration
- the need to use all your senses
- the importance that controlling speed has in dealing with hazards.

# Element E
## Practical on-road riding

This is the final element of the CBT course. You'll ride out on the road accompanied by, and in radio contact with, a certified trainer, possibly with one other trainee, for at least two hours.

You'll have to demonstrate that you can cope safely with a variety of road and traffic conditions.

Expect your trainer to stop occasionally to discuss some aspect of your riding and explain how to put the theory into practice.

Your ride should cover the topics discussed in this part of the book (some may not be covered because of the limits of the location).

Your riding will be constantly assessed by your trainer, who will sign a certificate of completion (DL196) when satisfied you're safe to continue learning alone.

Those who are profoundly deaf are exempt from the requirement to be in radio contact.

## Traffic lights

You **MUST** know how to act at traffic lights. Apart from knowing the sequence of lights, you need to know

- what the colours mean
- how to approach green lights safely
- how to cope with filter lanes
- what to do if traffic lights fail.

You'll also need to know about school crossing warning lights.

**Basic skills**  You must be able to approach traffic lights at the correct speed and react to the road and weather conditions and also react correctly to changing lights.

### Faults to avoid

- failing to stop at a red light
- approaching green traffic lights too fast
- proceeding into the junction when the green light shows but the way isn't clear
- hesitating as the green light changes and stopping unsafely.

*Knowing the sequence of traffic lights can help you plan ahead.*

---

### What's the sequence of the traffic lights?

**Red**  Stop and wait at the stop line.

**Red and amber**  Stop and wait. Don't go until green shows.

**Green**  Go, if it's safe.

**Amber**  Stop, unless you've already crossed the line or you're so close to it that pulling up might cause an incident.

---

## Roundabouts

There are set procedures for dealing with roundabouts. Your trainer should discuss and demonstrate how to go left, ahead and right.

This will involve learning how to apply the OSM/PSL routine for the direction you intend to travel. This will include

- signalling procedures
- lane discipline
- observation.

Your trainer will want to see you use the correct procedures for each roundabout you deal with.

**Basic skills** You must be able to

- take effective rear observation
- approach at the correct speed and judge the speed of other traffic
- give the correct signals at the right time and cancel them correctly
- follow the correct road position throughout.

**Faults to avoid**

- giving wrong or misleading signals
- approaching at the wrong speed
- stopping when the way is clear or riding out into the path of approaching traffic
- positioning incorrectly
- failing to take effective observation.

## Junctions

You'll have practised turning left and right in Element C. You'll now have to combine those riding skills with real traffic situations.

Your trainer will want to see you deal with a variety of junctions. These may include

- crossroads
- T-junctions
- staggered junctions
- Y-junctions.

You'll be expected to respond to signs such as

- warning signs
- 'stop' signs
- direction signs
- 'no entry' signs
- priority signs.

Don't forget to also take account of the road markings.

**Remember,** the road surface at junctions is often an additional hazard for motorcyclists. If you're riding on a shiny or loose surface don't

- **brake fiercely**
- **accelerate harshly.**

You must show that you're aware of other road users and watch for vehicles approaching, emerging or turning.

**Basic skills** To deal safely with junctions you must

- use the OSM/PSL routine correctly as you approach a junction
- position yourself correctly on the road
- control your speed to suit the road, weather and traffic conditions
- obey road signs and markings
- react correctly to other road users
- demonstrate effective observation.

*Your trainer will make sure you can deal safely with all types of junctions.*

### Faults to avoid

- stopping or waiting unnecessarily
- approaching a junction too fast
- overtaking as you approach a junction
- riding into a junction unsafely
- incorrect use of signals
- incorrect road position.

All junctions must be treated with great care.

*Zebra crossings have beacons to help you see the crossing from a distance.*

*Pelican, puffin, toucan and equestrian crossings are activated when someone pushes the button.*

## Pedestrian crossings

There's a variety of pedestrian crossings you may encounter. Your trainer will want to see you deal with crossings in the appropriate way

- **zebra crossings** slow down and be prepared to stop for waiting pedestrians

- **pelican and puffin crossings** always stop if the red light shows. You should also give way to pedestrians on a pelican crossing when the amber lights are flashing

- **toucan crossings** don't forget to give way to cyclists on a toucan crossing, as you would to pedestrians

- **equestrian crossings** remember that loud noises such as a horn or an engine revving can startle a horse into bolting or throwing its rider into the road. Take care when around animals.

**Basic skills** As you approach a crossing you need to

- control your speed
- react correctly to pedestrians waiting to cross
- know how and why you would give an arm signal as you stop at a zebra crossing.

### Faults to avoid

- approaching a crossing too fast
- failing to stop or show awareness of waiting pedestrians
- stopping across a crossing so blocking the way for pedestrians
- overtaking within the zigzag lines leading up to a crossing
- waving pedestrians across the road
- failing to respond correctly to traffic light signals at controlled crossings.

## Gradients

During this element your trainer will want to see that you can cope with gradients.

This will entail

- hill-start procedures
- riding uphill
- riding downhill.

You should have some understanding of how riding uphill or downhill can affect control of your motorcycle.

**Basic skills** To move off on an uphill gradient you need to have good control of the clutch and throttle.

When riding down a steep hill, you need to know how to control your speed using the brakes and gears.

### Faults to avoid

- moving off into the path of passing traffic
- stalling the engine
- rolling backwards.

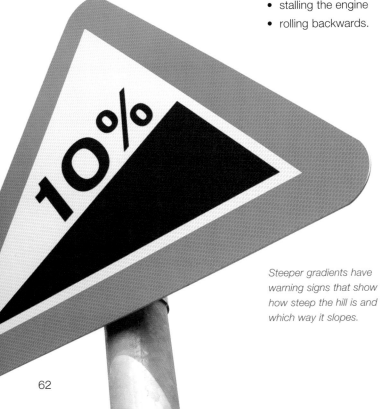

*Steeper gradients have warning signs that show how steep the hill is and which way it slopes.*

## Bends

Any bend can be a hazard. You must be able to recognise the hazard and deal with it safely.

Your trainer will want to see that you ride at a speed such that you can stop within the distance you can see and keep to the correct road position. Also that you're aware of road surface hazards such as drain covers, loose surfaces and adverse camber.

On left-hand bends you'll have less view ahead. Be prepared for pedestrians, stopped or broken-down vehicles, cyclists, and stationary vehicles waiting to turn right.

You should know how the weather affects your safety when cornering.

**Basic skills** To help you assess any bend, you should be looking out for road signs, road markings and chevrons.

When approaching a bend, you need to control your speed and select the correct gear, while leaving a safe gap between you and other vehicles. You must also be able to lean into a bend while steering a steady course.

### Faults to avoid

- braking while leaning over
- coasting
- cornering too fast
- leaning over too far
- riding too close to oncoming traffic or too close to the gutter.

*Your instructor will give you guidance to help you position correctly for right and left bends.*

*Advance warning triangles help you to plan ahead even though you may not be able to see the obstruction.*

*A bus is a large and obvious obstruction and its size could also make it easy to conceal people wanting to cross the road.*

## Obstructions

Obstructions are another hazard that you'll need to deal with.

To deal safely with these your trainer will want to see that you're riding defensively. That means always riding

- at the correct speed for the road, weather and traffic conditions
- in the correct position
- in the correct gear
- looking ahead, anticipating and preparing for changing situations.

**Basic skills** How well you cope with an obstruction depends largely on how well you plan ahead.

To cope with hazards you need to be

- looking well ahead
- giving yourself time and space to react
- using the OSM/PSL routine
- in the correct position
- in full control of your speed.

Your attitude can affect how easily you learn these skills.

**Faults to avoid**

- failing to look far enough ahead
- reacting too late
- riding too fast
- approaching an obstruction in the wrong gear.

## U-turn

As part of Element C you practised riding a U-turn on the training area. During this element you'll be expected to ride a U-turn on the road. This builds on the skills you learned earlier and helps prepare you for your practical motorcycle test.

Your trainer will find a quiet side road and explain what's required.

**Basic skills** You'll need to show that you've developed good balance and are skilled in the use of the clutch, throttle, rear brake and steering.

You'll have to develop these skills to include coping with

• the camber of the road

• the possibility of passing traffic

• kerbs on either side.

**Faults to avoid**

• failure to take effective observation before or during the exercise

• riding into the kerb or onto the pavement

• using your feet to help balance

• harsh, clumsy use of the clutch and throttle.

## Stopping as in an emergency

You've learnt and practised this exercise in Element C. In this element you repeat the exercise but in an on-road situation. This will

- develop your earlier skills
- help ensure your safety if an emergency does arise
- prepare you for performing this exercise on your practical motorcycle test.

Your trainer will find a quiet side road and explain the signal to be used. You'll then be expected to ride at normal speed before being given the signal to stop.

At no time will your trainer let you ride off out of sight.

**Basic skills**  You'll need to prove that you can do all of the following safely

- react quickly to the 'stop' signal
- use both brakes in the appropriate ratio
- quickly correct a locked wheel.

### Faults to avoid

- riding too slowly before the signal
- taking rear observation before reacting to the stop signal
- locking one or both wheels and failing to correct the fault
- stopping too slowly
- moving off unsafely after stopping.

# CBT record

| Name | | has satisfactorily completed: |
|------|---|------------------------------|

| | Signature of instructor | Date of completion |
|---|---|---|
| **Element A**<br>Introduction to CBT | | |
| **Element B**<br>Practical on-site training | | |
| **Element C**<br>Practical on-site riding | | |
| **Element D**<br>Practical on-road training | | |
| **Element E**<br>Practical on-road riding | | |
| Name of ATB | | |

## Using the record

You can use this log to record your progress through CBT. As you successfully complete each element get your trainer to sign this progress record.

This will give you

- a record of when you successfully complete each element
- a record of your trainer
- evidence of your progress to date.

# After CBT

CBT will give you the foundations on which to build a safe motorcycling career. However, like all new skills you need training and practice to become good at them.

## Training

Many ATBs provide additional training up to practical test standard. When you attend this training you may find that you're in a group with other learners.

There's a maximum ratio of four learners to each trainer for post-CBT training using learner machines.

Sometimes ATBs can book your theory and practical tests for you. Ask your trainer about further training and make sure the full syllabus is covered (see section 7).

## Practice

This is essential so that you practise

- on as many types of road as you can
- on dual carriageways where the national speed limit applies
- in all sorts of conditions (even in darkness).

You'll be asked to ride on a variety of road types during the on-road test module. Don't just concentrate on roads near the test centre or the exercises included in the tests. When you practise try not to

- obstruct other traffic. Most drivers are tolerant of learners, but don't try their patience too much
- annoy local residents, for example, by practising emergency stops in quiet residential streets.

*In busy urban conditions you may have to consider many hazards close together. Prioritising hazards is a skill that develops with practice.*

*Rural roads present some unique hazards but concentration and good forward planning should enable you to deal with them safely.*

# section **three**
# BEFORE YOUR TESTS

This section covers

- Booking your tests
- Your theory test
- Theory into practice
- The practical tests
- Your test motorcycle

# Booking your tests

Some ATBs will be able to book your theory and practical tests for you. Alternatively, you can book your tests online, by telephone, or by post as explained below.

## Booking online or by telephone

You can book theory and practical tests by either of these methods and you'll be given the date and time of your test immediately. You can book online at **www.gov.uk**

To book by telephone, call 0300 200 1122. If you're a Welsh speaker call 0300 200 1133. If you're deaf and need a minicom machine call 0300 200 1166 for theory tests and 0300 200 1144 for practical tests.

To book in Northern Ireland call 0845 600 6700 for theory tests and 0870 247 2472 for practical tests.

When booking you'll need to identify what sort of test you want to book and provide

- your driver number (from your licence)
- credit or debit card details. Please note that the person who books the test must be the card holder
- if booking a practical test you'll need your theory test pass certificate number.

## Booking by post

Fill in the application form for the type of test you wish to take and send it, together with the correct fee, to the address shown on the back of the form. You can get application forms from driving test centres or ask your ATB.

You may pay by cheque, postal order or with credit/debit card. Please don't send cash. You'll receive an appointment email/ letter within 10 days.

*The easiest way to book your test is online. Simply visit* **www.gov.uk**

## Appointment confirmation

Your confirmation will be sent in the post if you don't have an email address.

## Disabilities or special needs

Whichever test you book, you need to let them know if you have a disability or if there are any other special circumstances. You'll still take the same type of test as every other test candidate, but more time may be allowed for the test.

To make sure enough time is allowed, it would help DSA to know if you

• are deaf or have severe hearing difficulties

• are in any way restricted in your movements

• have any disability that may affect your riding.

If you can't speak English or are deaf, you're allowed to bring an interpreter (this can be your trainer if you wish). The interpreter must be 16 years or over.

### How much do the tests cost?

Your ATB should be able to tell you or you can find out from **www.gov.uk** or by calling 0300 200 1122.

### Can I take my tests on a weekend or in the evening?

Theory tests are available on some weekday evenings and Saturdays while practical tests are available at some test centres on Saturdays, Sundays and in the summer, on weekday evenings. The fee for practical tests taken outside normal working hours is higher than during normal working hours on weekdays.

### How do I change or cancel my test appointment?

You can change or cancel your test appointment online at **www.gov.uk**. Alternatively, you can change or cancel a test appointment by calling 0300 200 1122.

You need to give at least three clear working days' notice for change or cancellation of a theory test or practical module, not counting the day DSA receive your request and the day of the test (Saturday is counted as a working day). If you don't give enough notice you'll lose your fee.

# Your theory test

*At theory test centres, lockers are provided for your personal possessions.*

*Your result should be available within 10 minutes of completing the test.*

The theory test will gauge your knowledge and understanding of riding theory and hazard perception.

A sound knowledge of the theory is essential to a better understanding of practical riding skills.

## Who's affected?

All motorcycle test candidates will have to pass the theory test before a booking for a practical test will be accepted. However, you won't have to take a theory test if you hold a full moped licence obtained by passing both a theory and practical moped test or are upgrading your motorcycle licence from an A1 to A2 or A2 to category A.

## Ready for your test?

If you're well prepared you shouldn't find the questions difficult. *The Official DSA Theory Test for Motorcyclists* is available as a book or on DVD-ROM and it contains comprehensive information about the test and all the revision questions, answers and explanations.

Study your copy of The Highway Code and the publications *The Official DSA Guide to Riding – the essential skills* and *Know Your Traffic Signs*. Always make sure that you have the most up-to-date versions of these books.

It's very important that you know and understand why the answers to the multiple choice questions are correct. Take this knowledge and put it into practice on the road. Your examiner will expect you to demonstrate what you've learned through your riding.

## Hazard perception

We strongly recommend that you use *The Official DSA Guide to Hazard Perception (DVD)*, preferably with your trainer, to prepare for the hazard perception part of the theory test.

The DVD is packed with useful tips, quizzes and expert advice. It also includes interactive hazard perception clips and your performance will receive a score so you'll know if you're ready to pass.

## On the day

The test centre staff will check your documents. You'll have to show your driving licence, and if your licence doesn't show your photograph you'll also have to show your passport (your passport doesn't have to be British). No other form of identification is acceptable.

Other forms of identification may be acceptable in Northern Ireland, please check **dvani.gov.uk** or refer to your test appointment letter.

*All documents must be original. We can't accept photocopies.*

Arrive in plenty of time so that you're not rushed. If you arrive late you may not be allowed to take the test.

## If you pass

The result should be available within 10 minutes of completing your test. If you've passed you'll be issued with a pass certificate that will be valid for two years.

## If you fail

If you haven't passed the theory test then you must retake it. You'll have to wait a minimum of three clear working days before you take the test again.

*It's important that you study, not just to pass the test, but to become a safer rider.*

# Theory into practice

Your theory test pass certificate is valid for two years and you must take it with you when you go for your practical tests. You must take and pass both practical test modules before your theory test pass certificate expires or you'll have to take the theory test again plus both modules of the practical test to gain a full licence.

When you take your practical test you must satisfy your examiner that you've fully understood everything that you learned for the theory test. The aspects are

- alertness and concentration
- courtesy and consideration
- care in the use of the controls to reduce mechanical wear and tear
- awareness of stopping distances and safety margins in all conditions
- hazard awareness

- correct action concerning pedestrians and other vulnerable road users
- dealing with other types of vehicle in the correct manner
- rules regarding speed limits and stopping restrictions
- road and traffic signs.

You'll also be expected to know

- the law regarding you and your vehicle
- what to do in the event of an accident
- the effect that extra loads have on your vehicle
- the effect that motoring has on the environment
- how to carry out simple safety checks on your vehicle.

# The practical tests

## About the practical tests

The practical test is split into two separate modules. A full motorcycling licence will only be issued when both modules have been passed.

**Module 1** is an off-road, specified manoeuvring test including an avoidance exercise, a U-turn, a slow ride and a controlled stop (see page 81).

**Module 2** is a road riding test including an eyesight test, two questions about carrying out safety checks on the vehicle and a question about balance when carrying a pillion passenger.

Your examiner will follow you on a motorcycle or occasionally in a car. You'll be fitted with earphones under your helmet and a radio receiver on a waist belt. This will enable you to hear the examiner's directions while riding on the road. You'll be given directions clearly and in good time.

You should ride in the way you've been taught by your trainer.

You must

- hold a current theory test pass before either module can be taken
- pass Module 1 before taking Module 2
- use the same category of motorcycle for both Modules 1 and 2

**Module 1 Pass Certificate**  If you pass Module 1, you'll be given a Module 1 Pass Certificate. This will show the category of motorcycle you used. Keep it safe as you'll have to show it to your examiner when you attend for Module 2.

You'll pass both modules if you show your examiner that you can

- complete the off-road specified manoeuvres
- ride safely and competently throughout
- demonstrate through your riding that you have a thorough knowledge of The Highway Code.

### How long will the modules last?

Module 1 will last about 20 minutes while Module 2 will last about 50 minutes.

### Are examiners supervised?

Examiners are frequently supervised by a senior officer. If a senior officer is present at your test, don't worry. They're only there to check that your examiner is testing you properly and won't interfere with the test or the result. They're not there to test you in any way.

### Does the standard of the test vary?

No. All examiners are trained to carry out tests to the same standard. Test routes are as uniform as possible and include a range of typical road and traffic conditions.

**How the examiner records faults**

Total  S  D

① ② ③④

Total faults  ⑤

① **Riding fault** A less serious fault, but an accumulation of these may result in failure

② **Area total** The number of riding faults made in one area

③ **Serious fault** Committing one of these will result in failure

④ **Dangerous fault** Committing one of these will result in failure

⑤ **Overall total** The total number of riding faults made in all areas during the test

## Documents

Take your appointment card with you and for both Modules 1 and 2 you'll have to show your

- driving licence, and if your licence doesn't show your photograph you'll also have to show your passport (your passport doesn't have to be British).
- theory test pass certificate
- CBT completion certificate unless you're upgrading your full motorcycle entitlement.

No other form of identification is acceptable. Other forms of identification may be acceptable in Northern Ireland, please check **dvani.gov.uk** or refer to your test appointment letter.

When attending for Module 2, you'll also have to show your Module 1 Pass Certificate.

## How you'll be assessed

Your examiner will assess any errors you make and, depending on their degree of seriousness, record them on the Riding Test Report form (DL25MC). You'll fail your test if you commit a serious or dangerous fault. You'll also fail if you commit more than a fixed number of riding faults. The examiner will use the following criteria

**Riding fault** Less serious, but has been assessed as such because of circumstances at that particular time. An accumulation of more than a fixed number of riding faults will result in a fail.

**Serious fault** Recorded when a potentially dangerous incident has occurred or a habitual riding fault indicates a serious weakness in your riding.

**Dangerous fault** Recorded when a fault is assessed as having caused actual danger.

At the end of the test, you'll be offered some general guidance to explain your riding test report.

## Are you ready?

If you've taken additional training, be guided by your trainer, who has the knowledge and experience to tell you when you're ready for each module.

For Module 1 you should be able to complete the manoeuvres consistently well while for Module 2 you must be able to ride with confidence and without assistance or guidance from your trainer.

If you can't, waiting until you're ready will save you time and money.

## Can anyone accompany me on the test?

If you need an interpreter you should notify DSA in advance and arrange for the interpreter to meet you at the test centre. Your interpreter must be 16 years or over and can be your trainer if you wish.

The Data Protection Act prevents your trainer from talking to your examiner about your practical test without your permission. If you didn't pass your test and want your trainer to help you understand the reason(s) why, your trainer needs to be on hand at the end of the test to listen to the debrief that the examiner will offer you. Tell the examiner that you would like your trainer to be present. This can help your trainer to plan any further training that you might need.

## When you've passed both modules

You'll be allowed to ride without L plates, unsupervised and on motorways.

The size of motorcycle you'll be licensed to ride immediately after passing your tests will depend on the machine you've used to take the test. See the next page for test motorcycle requirements.

# Your test motorcycle

**Important** You must use the same category of motorcycle for both practical test modules.

**Legally roadworthy** Your machine must have a current test certificate, if it's over the prescribed age.

**Insurance** You must be fully covered by insurance for you to ride on the date of your test and for its present use.

**Size and power** Ensure that your machine has the correct engine size/power output for the category of test that you're taking.

**Licence** Make sure that your motorcycle is properly licensed with the correct tax disc on display.

**L plates** The red L plates (or D plates in Wales) fitted to your bike must be visible from the front and rear.

If you overlook any of these your test may be cancelled and you could lose your fee.

**Mopeds** Any motorcycle with an engine smaller than 50 cc is classed as a moped. If you pass your test on a moped, you'll gain a category P licence.

# section **four**

# THE PRACTICAL RIDING TEST

## off-road module

This section covers

- The off-road module
- The off-road manoeuvring area
- Before you start the engine
- Using the stand and manual handling
- Slalom and figure of eight
- Slow ride
- U-turn
- Cornering and controlled stopping
- Cornering and the emergency stop
- Cornering and the avoidance exerci
- Other machines

# The off-road module

The off-road module of the practical motorcycle test has to be successfully completed before the accompanied on-road module can be taken.

At the beginning of the test your examiner will ask you to

- sign the declaration on the Riding Test Report form (DL25MC)
- show your documents (see page 77).

You'll then be asked to ride your motorcycle onto the motorcycle manoeuvring area. When on the area, behave as if you're riding on the public road, which should include any necessary safety checks, and avoid making contact with any of the marker cones.

Your examiner will ask you to push or ride your motorcycle forwards into one of the bays formed by marker cones and put it on its stand.

The off-road element includes

- using the stand
- manual handling
- slalom and figure of eight
- slow ride
- U-turn
- cornering with a controlled stop
- cornering with an emergency stop
- cornering with an avoidance exercise.

Your examiner will explain each exercise to you using a diagram (see page 82) to describe the requirements.

Riders who commit faults of a serious or dangerous nature during the off-road element won't pass the test. The hill start, angle start and normal stop exercises will continue to be tested during the on-road module.

# The off-road manoeuvring area

## Left circuit (the right circuit mirrors this layout)

### Key

1 Stands and manual handling
2 Slalom
3 Figure of eight
4 Slow ride
5 U-turn
6 Cornering
7 Controlled stop
8 30 km/h (19 mph) circuit ride
9 50 km/h (32 mph) emergency brake
10 30 km/h (19 mph) circuit ride
11 50 km/h (32 mph) avoidance

### Mopeds

For all mopeds, speed requirements are 30 kph/19 mph.

Diagram for illustrative purposes only. For details of the circuit measurements, see the information about the motorcycle practical riding test at **www.gov.uk**

Please note if you're taking your off-road module on a casual hire site, VOSA site or in Northern Ireland, the circuit layout may vary in shape, although the manoeuvres are the same. For further details please speak to your trainer or visit **www.gov.uk** or for Northern Ireland **dvani.gov.uk/**

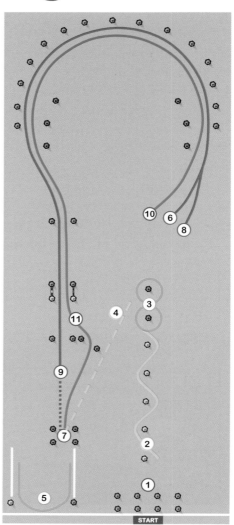

# Before you start the engine

## What the test requires

Before you start the engine you must always check that

- the fuel tap is turned on
- the engine kill switch is in the 'on' position
- the gear lever is in neutral.

Many road safety organisations recommend that you use dipped headlights at all times. **Be seen, be safe.**

**Faults to avoid**  You shouldn't

- use the fuel tap's reserve position instead of the 'on' position. The motorcycle will run normally but you'll have no warning when your fuel is running low.
- attempt to start the engine in gear with the clutch engaged.

# Using the stand and manual handling

## What the test requires

You'll be required to demonstrate that you can take the motorcycle off the stand and wheel it backwards from one bay to another without the use of the engine. You may choose to wheel it backwards in an arc from one bay to the other or you may elect to wheel it backwards out of the first bay before pushing it forwards and then backwards into the adjacent bay.

When you've wheeled it into the adjacent bay, you'll have to put it back on its stand.

## How your examiner will test you

When taking your motorcycle off its stand or when wheeling it you must

- make any necessary safety checks
- retain your balance and full control.

Paddling or sitting astride the machine to move it isn't allowed other than by candidates with special needs such as those with

- limited mobility
- restricted leg movement.

When putting your motorcycle onto its stand you may use either the side or the centre stand. A motorcycle with no stand isn't suitable for the test.

**Faults to avoid**  You shouldn't

- omit necessary safety checks
- lose control
- lose your balance
- set the stand incorrectly
- position the motorcycle inaccurately
- make contact with a marker cone.

# Slalom and figure of eight

## What the test requires

You'll be asked to ride a slalom and a figure of eight. This is to demonstrate your ability to ride and steer your motorcycle slowly while manoeuvring in a restricted space under control. You should maintain a reasonable degree of slow speed control and balance throughout the exercise.

## How your examiner will test you

Effective safety checks should be taken before starting the exercise. Your examiner will look for skilled use of the

- throttle
- clutch
- rear brake

so that you can

- steer accurately between the marker cones
- keep your balance

at the low speed necessary to complete the exercise.

The slalom exercise will lead into two circuits of the figure of eight.

**Faults to avoid** You shouldn't

- omit necessary safety checks before moving away
- lose control of the motorcycle
- come into contact with a marker cone
- lose control of your speed.

# Slow ride

## What the test requires

You'll be asked to demonstrate your ability to ride slowly, in a straight line, as if in slow-moving traffic.

## How your examiner will test you

Effective safety checks should be taken before you move away. Your examiner will look for skilled use of the throttle, clutch and rear brake so that you can

- ride slowly
- ride in a reasonably straight line.

**Faults to avoid**  You shouldn't

- omit necessary safety checks before moving away
- lose control of your machine
- ride too fast.

# U-turn

## What the test requires

You'll be asked to ride a U-turn between two lines representing either side of a public road.

## How your examiner will test you

Effective safety checks should be taken before you move away and before you turn. Your examiner will look for skilled use of the throttle, clutch and rear brake so that you can

- turn your machine round under control and accurately between the lines
- keep your balance.

**Faults to avoid** You shouldn't

- omit necessary safety checks before moving away
- omit necessary safety checks before turning
- lose control of the machine
- ride on or over the lines.

# Cornering and controlled stopping

## What the test requires

You'll be asked to ride a left or right circuit, at the examiner's discretion, and to control your motorcycle safely and then bring it to a controlled halt in an area formed by marker cones.

There's no minimum speed requirement for this exercise, although you'll be asked to try and reach a speed of between 30–50 km/h (20–30 mph) as you pass the speed measuring equipment.

## How your examiner will test you

Effective safety checks should be taken before starting the exercise. Your examiner will look for skilled use of the controls so that you can

- enter, ride around and leave the bend under control
- bring your machine to a stop accurately and under full control.

**Faults to avoid**  You shouldn't

- omit necessary safety checks before moving away
- come into contact with any marker cones
- stop outside the area formed by marker cones.

# Cornering and the emergency stop

## What the test requires

You'll be required to demonstrate your ability to stop as quickly and safely as possible while retaining full control of your motorcycle. You'll be asked to ride a left or right circuit. If you reach a speed of around 30 km/h (about 19 mph) while riding round the bend it will help you reach the minimum speed required of 50 km/h (about 32 mph) as you pass the speed measuring device. Soon after you pass the speed measuring device your examiner will give you a signal to stop, as in an emergency. The signal will be demonstrated before you begin.

## How your examiner will test you

Effective safety checks should be taken before starting the exercise. Your examiner will look for skilled use of the

- throttle
- clutch
- gears
- front and rear brakes

so that you can

- enter and leave the bend under control and with accuracy

- respond promptly to the signal to stop given by the examiner
- apply maximum braking and bring your machine to a stop under full control.

The speed measuring device will accurately record your speed before you carry out the emergency stop.

**Faults to avoid**  You shouldn't

- omit necessary safety checks before moving away
- come into contact with any marker cones
- lock a wheel while braking
- lose control of the machine.

If you ride too slowly and don't achieve the minimum speed requirement your examiner may allow you to repeat the exercise.

If a serious or dangerous fault occurs during this exercise you won't be asked to carry out the avoidance exercise.

# Cornering and the avoidance exercise

## What the test requires

You'll be asked to ride a left or right circuit, at the examiner's discretion. If you reach a speed of around 30 km/h (about 19 mph) while riding round the bend it will help you reach the minimum speed required of 50 km/h (about 32 mph) as you pass the speed measuring device. When you've passed the speed measuring device, you'll be required to control your motorcycle safely while steering to avoid a stationary obstacle and then bring it to a controlled halt in an area formed by marker cones.

## How your examiner will test you

Effective safety checks should be taken before starting the exercise. Your examiner will look for skilled use of the

- throttle
- clutch
- gears
- front brake
- rear brake

so that you can

- enter and leave the bend under control and with accuracy

- meet the minimum speed requirement before avoiding an obstacle
- steer accurately between marker cones
- bring your motorcycle safely to a controlled halt with the front wheel within a box formed by marker cones.

The speed measuring device will accurately record your speed before you carry out the avoidance exercise.

**Faults to avoid**  You shouldn't

- omit necessary safety checks before moving away
- come into contact with any marker cones
- lock a wheel while braking
- stop inaccurately.

If you ride too slowly and don't achieve the minimum speed requirement your examiner may allow you to repeat the exercise.

# Other machines

## Mopeds

The left or right circuit ride, avoidance and emergency stop exercise will be carried out at a minimum speed of 30 km/h (about 19 mph). All other aspects of the test remain the same.

## Combination sidecars

These vehicles can only be used if you have a physical disability. You won't be required to carry out the

- exercise using the stand
- wheeling exercises
- avoidance exercise.

Additional time will be allowed for your test to be conducted. Non-disabled candidates may not use combination sidecars for their test.

The examiner's decision on whether to use a left or right circuit will be based on the

characteristics of the outfit. If the sidecar is positioned on the left of the machine a right-handed circuit will be used and vice versa.

The examiner will make adjustments to the slalom marker cones to accommodate the extra width of the vehicle. The width between the cones associated with the speed measuring device and the controlled stopping box will be increased to 1.5 times the width of the outfit.

The U-turn may be carried out from either left to right or right to left.

## Category B1 vehicles

Licence categories are changing from 19 January 2013 and we will no longer be offering a test on vehicles that remain in the B1 category. After this date, any vehicle that remains in category B1 can only be driven on a full car licence under the category B entitlement. For more information, visit **www.gov.uk**

Drivers holding B1 entitlement before this date won't be affected.

# section **five**
# THE PRACTICAL RIDING TEST
## on-road module

This section covers
- The on-road module
- The eyesight test
- Safety checks and balance question
- The motorcycle controls
- Moving off
- Rear observation
- Giving signals
- Acting on signs and signals
- Use of speed
- Making progress
- Hazards – the correct routine
- Junctions and roundabouts
  - Overtaking
    - Meeting and passing other vehicles
      - Crossing the path of other vehicles
        - Following behind at a safe distance
          - Positioning and lane discipline
            - Pedestrian crossings
            - Selecting a safe place to stop
              - Awareness and anticipation
            - Independent riding
  - If you don't pass
  - If you pass both module

# The on-road module

You must pass both the off-road and on-road modules within two years of passing your theory test. In addition you must hold a current CBT completion certificate when taking both modules.

Your examiner will be understanding and sympathetic and will make every effort to put you at ease.

At the beginning of the on-road module your examiner will ask you to

- sign the declaration on the Riding Test Report form (DL25MC)
- show your documents (see page 77).

You'll then be fitted with the radio system. Your examiner will explain how directions will be given and check that the radio equipment is working. You'll then be directed by your examiner who will follow on a motorcycle or in a car.

## The test

The test itself has many elements. It covers

- the eyesight test
- safety check and balance questions
- your use of the controls
- moving off
- rear observation
- giving signals
- acting on road signs and signals
- use of speed
- making progress
- hazards
- junctions and roundabouts
- overtaking
- meeting and passing other vehicles
- crossing the path of other vehicles
- following at a safe distance
- positioning and lane discipline
- pedestrian crossings
- selecting a safe place to stop
- awareness and anticipation
- independent riding.

**Angle start** Your examiner will ask you to pull up just before a parked vehicle. Before you move off, make sure that you check

- to the rear and into the blind area
- ahead to see there's no danger from approaching traffic.

If an angle start occurs normally during the test, you may not be asked to do it again.

**Hill start** Your examiner may ask you to pull up on an uphill gradient.

When moving away, your machine could be slower to accelerate. You'll need to remember this when judging the moment to ride on.

You'll also need to balance brakes, clutch and throttle to ensure a smooth move off without

- stalling the engine
- rolling backwards.

# The eyesight test

## What the test requires

You must satisfy your examiner that, in good daylight, you can read a vehicle number plate at a minimum distance of 20 metres (about 66 feet).

Number plates in the older format (X123XXX) have a wider font and should be read from a distance of 20.5 metres (about 67 feet).

*You'll be asked to read a clean number plate in good daylight.*

If you need glasses or contact lenses to read the number plate, that's fine. However, you **MUST** wear them during the test and whenever you ride.

If you've had sight correction surgery you should declare this when you apply for your provisional licence.

## How your examiner will test you

Before you begin riding, your examiner will point out a vehicle and ask you to read its number plate.

> **Remember,** if you normally wear glasses or contact lenses, always wear them whenever you ride.

If you can't speak English or have difficulty reading, you may copy down what you see.

If your answer is incorrect, your examiner will measure the exact distance and repeat the test.

## Failing the eyesight test

If you can't demonstrate to your examiner that your eyesight is up to the required standard

• you will have failed your motorcycle test

• your test will go no further.

# Safety checks and balance question

## What the test requires

You must satisfy the examiner that you can prepare to ride safely by carrying out basic safety checks on the motorcycle you're using on the test.

You'll be expected to know how to carry out checks relating to

- tyres
- brakes
- fluids
- lights
- reflectors
- direction indicators
- horn.

You must also know how balance will be affected when carrying a pillion passenger.

## How your examiner will test you

At the start of the test the examiner will ask you to explain and demonstrate how you would carry out certain safety checks.

In addition your examiner will ask you one question about balance when carrying a pillion passenger.

The examiner wants to see that you're familiar with the motorcycle you're using for the test.

They'll want you to explain, and in some cases demonstrate, how you would carry out basic safety checks on the motorcycle you're using on the test.

## Questions you could be asked

The examiner could ask you about checking

- tyres for correct pressure and condition
- brakes for working order before any journey
- fluid levels (including engine oil, brake fluid and, on a motorcycle with a liquid cooled engine, coolant) – where they are and how you would check the levels
- reflectors and lights (including brake lights and direction indicators) for good working order and visibility
- the drive chain (if fitted) for wear, lubrication and tension
- the engine kill switch

- other components (including steering, horn and warning devices) for good working order.

There's a limited number of safety check questions that you can be asked on test. They'll mostly take the form of 'show me' or 'tell me' questions.

For a list of all the safety questions you could be asked by the examiner, see the information about the motorcycle practical riding test at **www.gov.uk**

**Faults you should avoid**

- Being unable to explain or demonstrate basic safety checks on the motorcycle you're using for the test.
- Being unable to explain how balance can be affected when carrying the additional weight of a pillion passenger.

# The motorcycle controls

## What the test requires

You should understand the functions of all switches that have a bearing on road safety such as your indicators, horn and lights. You should know where to find these switches on the motorcycle you're riding.

You should also understand the meaning of gauges or other instruments including the speedometer and various warning lights.

You're also required to know the functions of all controls including

- throttle
- clutch
- front and rear brake
- steering
- gears.

You should use these controls

- smoothly
- competently
- safely
- at the right time.

**If you're riding an automatic** Make sure that you fully understand the controls before you attempt to ride a motorcycle with automatic transmission.

## Throttle and clutch

You should

- balance the throttle and clutch to pull away smoothly
- accelerate gradually to gain speed
- pull the clutch in just before the motorcycle stops.

If you're riding a motorcycle with automatic or semi-automatic transmission, you should ensure that the brakes are used to prevent creeping forward and control the throttle when moving off and changing gear.

**Faults to avoid** Don't accelerate fiercely. This can lead to a loss of control and may distract or alarm other road users.

Avoid using the clutch in a jerky and uncontrolled manner when moving off or changing gear.

## Brakes

You should use both brakes correctly and in good time. You should brake lightly in most situations.

**Faults to avoid** You shouldn't brake harshly, except in an emergency. Don't use either the front or rear brake alone.

*You should understand all the instruments and know what to do if a warning light is showing.*

## Gears

You should choose the right gear for your speed and road conditions. Change gear in good time so that you're ready for a hazard or junction.

**Faults to avoid**  You shouldn't

- select the wrong gear
- coast with the clutch lever pulled in or the gear lever in neutral.

## Steering

You should keep both hands on the handlebars and make sure your steering movements are steady and smooth.

Always begin turning at the correct time when negotiating a corner and show awareness of the road surface.

**Faults to avoid**  Don't turn too early when steering around a corner. If you do, you risk

- cutting the corner when turning right and putting others at risk
- striking the kerb when turning left.

Don't turn too late. You could put other road users at risk by swinging wide on left turns and overshooting right turns.

You shouldn't brake and steer together, lean the motorcycle over too far and cause one or both tyres to lose their grip, or move out before turning left.

# Moving off

## What the test requires

You should be able to move off safely and under control both on the flat and on a hill, where appropriate. You'll also have to demonstrate moving off from behind a parked car.

## How your examiner will test you

Your examiner will watch your use of the controls and observation of other road users each time you move off.

Use your mirrors and signal if necessary. Look around over your shoulder and check any blind spots that can't be seen in your mirror. Move off under control making balanced use of the controls and using the correct gear.

*Before moving off, you'll need to look around and check for hazards that would not be visible in your mirrors.*

**Angle start**  Your examiner will ask you to pull up just before a parked vehicle. Before you move off, make sure that you check

- to the rear and into the blind area
- ahead to see there's no danger from approaching traffic.

If an angle start occurs normally during the test, you may not be asked to do it again.

**Hill start**  Your examiner might ask you to pull up on an uphill gradient.

When moving off, your machine could be slower to accelerate. You'll need to remember this when judging the moment to ride off.

**Faults to avoid**  You shouldn't

- immediately signal without first taking effective observation around you
- pull out without looking
- cause other road users to stop or alter their course
- accelerate excessively
- move off in too high a gear
- fail to coordinate the controls correctly and stall the engine.

# Rear observation

*Looking around while moving needs to be timed carefully and performed without affecting the steering.*

## What the test requires

Make sure that you take effective rear observation

- before any manoeuvre
- to keep aware of what's happening behind you.

Check carefully before

- moving off
- signalling
- changing direction
- turning to the left or right
- overtaking or changing lanes
- increasing speed
- slowing down or stopping.

## How your examiner will test you

Your examiner will watch your use of rear observation as you ride. Use the OSM routine. You should

- look before you signal
- look and signal before you act
- act sensibly and safely on what you see when you've taken rear observation.

You should be aware that the mirrors won't show everything behind you (see page 42 for more information about blind spots).

**Faults to avoid** You shouldn't manoeuvre without taking rear observation or fail to act on what you see behind.

# Giving signals

## What the test requires

You should signal

- to let others know what you intend to do
- to help other road users, including pedestrians
- in plenty of time.

You must only use the signals shown in The Highway Code.

Your signals should help other road users

- to understand what you intend to do
- to react safely.

Always make sure that your signal is cancelled after use.

## How your examiner will test you

Your examiner will watch carefully how you use your signals as you ride.

Give signals clearly and in good time.

You should also know how to give arm signals and when they're necessary.

**Faults to avoid**  You shouldn't

- give signals carelessly
- mislead other road users
- forget to cancel the signal
- wave at pedestrians to cross the road.

# Acting on signs and signals

## What the test requires

You should be able to understand all traffic signs and road markings. You must also react to them in good time.

At the beginning of the test your examiner will ask you to follow the road ahead.

You'll be asked to turn at junctions, but look out for lane markings and direction signs. You'll be expected to act on these.

**Traffic lights** You **MUST** act correctly at traffic lights. When the green light shows, check that the road is clear before proceeding.

**Signals by authorised persons** You **MUST** obey the signals given by

- police officers
- traffic wardens
- school crossing patrols
- Highways Agency traffic officers and Vehicle and Operator Services Agency officers.

**Traffic calming measures** Take particular care on roads which have been altered by the addition of

- 20 mph speed limit zones
- speed restriction humps
- width restrictions marked by bollards, posts or paved areas.

# Use of speed

## What the test requires

You should make good progress along the road bearing in mind

- road conditions
- traffic conditions
- weather conditions
- road signs and speed limits.

## How your examiner will test you

Your examiner will watch carefully your control of speed as you ride. You should

- take great care in the use of speed
- make sure that you can stop safely, well within the distance you can see to be clear

- leave a safe distance between yourself and other vehicles
- leave extra distance on wet or slippery roads
- approach junctions and hazards at the correct speed.

**Faults to avoid** You shouldn't

- ride too fast for the road and traffic conditions
- change your speed unpredictably.

# Making progress

## What the test requires

You should

- make reasonable progress along the road
- ride at a speed appropriate to road and traffic conditions
- move off at junctions as soon as it's safe to do so.

## How your examiner will test you

Your examiner will watch your riding and will want to see you

- make reasonable progress along the road
- keep up with traffic
- show confidence, together with sound judgement
- comply with the speed limits.

You should be able to choose the correct speed for the

- type of road
- road surface
- type and density of traffic
- weather and visibility.

**Faults to avoid** You shouldn't

- ride too slowly, holding up other traffic
- be over-cautious or stop and wait when it's safe to go
- prepare too early for junctions by approaching too slowly and holding up traffic.

> **Remember,** you should approach all hazards at a safe speed.

# Hazards – the correct routine

## What's a hazard?

A hazard is any situation that could involve adjusting speed or altering course. Look well ahead where there are

- road junctions or roundabouts
- parked vehicles
- cyclists or horse riders
- pedestrian crossings.

By identifying the hazard early you'll have time to take the appropriate action.

You may have to deal with several hazards at once or during a short space of time. This may mean using your initiative and common sense to deal with the particular circumstances.

## What the test requires

Always use the OSM/PSL routine when approaching a hazard.

**Observation**  Check the position of following traffic using your mirrors or by looking behind at an appropriate time.

**Signal**  If necessary, signal your intention to change course or slow down. Signal clearly and in good time.

**Manoeuvre**  A manoeuvre is any change of speed or position, from slowing or stopping to turning off a busy road. Manoeuvre has three phases: position, speed, then look. You should consider each phase in turn and use them as appropriate.

# Junctions and roundabouts

## What the test requires

You should

- use the OSM routine when you approach a junction or a roundabout
- position your motorcycle correctly. Adjust your speed and stop if necessary
- use the correct lane if the road has lane markings. In a one-way street choose that lane as soon as you can do so safely.

If the road has no lane markings, when turning left, keep to the left.

Watch out for

- cyclists
- pedestrians crossing.

When turning right, you should

- keep as close to the centre of the road as is safe
- use effective observation before you enter a junction
- take a 'lifesaver' check over your right shoulder before you turn.

*Your examiner will give you directions in good time and will watch your OSM routine as you approach junctions.*

*Your examiner will assess your positioning and use of signals at roundabouts.*

## How your examiner will test you

Your examiner will watch carefully and take account of your

- use of the OSM/PSL routine
- position and speed on approach to the hazard
- observation and judgement.

You should be able to

- observe road signs and markings and act correctly on what you see
- judge the correct speed on approach to the hazard

- slow down in good time, without harsh braking
- judge the speed of the other traffic, especially at roundabouts and when you're joining major roads
- position and turn correctly.

**Faults to avoid**  You shouldn't

- approach the junction at the wrong speed
- position and turn incorrectly
- enter a junction unsafely
- stop or wait unnecessarily.

# Overtaking

## What the test requires

When overtaking you must

- observe any signs and road markings which prohibit overtaking
- allow enough room
- give cyclists and horses at least as much room as a car. Cyclists might swerve or wobble and a startled horse can shy or jump unpredictably
- allow enough space after overtaking. Don't cut in.

*If you need to overtake use the OSM/PSL routine. Don't overtake when approaching a junction as the driver could be turning right and may not be aware of you.*

## How your examiner will test you

Your examiner will watch and take into account how you

- use the OSM/PSL routine
- react to road and traffic conditions
- handle the controls.

You should be able to judge the speed and position of vehicles

- behind, which might be trying to overtake you
- in front, if you're planning to overtake
- coming towards you.

Overtake only when you can do so

- safely
- without causing other vehicles to slow down or alter course.

**Faults to avoid** You shouldn't overtake when

- your view of the road ahead isn't clear
- you would have to exceed the speed limit
- there's oncoming traffic and you're squeezing between the oncoming traffic and the vehicle you're overtaking
- the road is narrow.

# Meeting and passing other vehicles

## What the test requires

You should deal with oncoming traffic safely and confidently. This applies on narrow roads and where there are parked cars or other obstructions.

If there's an obstruction on your side of the road, or not enough space for two vehicles to pass safely, you should use the OSM/PSL routine and be prepared to give way to oncoming traffic.

If you need to stop, keep well back from the obstruction to give yourself

- a better view of the road ahead
- room to move off easily when the road is clear.

When you're passing parked cars, allow at least the width of a car door, if possible.

## How your examiner will test you

Your examiner will watch carefully and take into account how you

- use the OSM/PSL routine
- react to road and traffic conditions
- handle the controls.

*Be patient. Don't be tempted to squeeze through small gaps.*

You should

- show judgement and control when meeting oncoming traffic
- be decisive when stopping and moving off
- allow enough room when passing parked cars.

**Watch out for**

- doors opening
- children running out into the road
- pedestrians stepping out from the pavement
- vehicles pulling out without warning.

# Crossing the path of other vehicles

## What the test requires

You should be able to cross the path of other vehicles safely and with confidence.

You normally need to cross the path of other vehicles when you have to turn right into a side road or driveway. You should

- use the OSM/PSL routine
- position correctly and adjust your speed
- watch out for oncoming traffic and stop if necessary.

Watch out for pedestrians crossing the side road or on the pavement, if you're entering a driveway.

## How your examiner will test you

Your examiner will watch carefully and take account of your judgement of the oncoming traffic.

You should show that you can turn right into a junction or driveway safely, using the OSM/PSL routine.

**Faults to avoid** You shouldn't cause other vehicles to slow down, change direction or stop.

You shouldn't

- turn too early and cut the corner
- leave it too late before you start to turn.

# Following behind at a safe distance

## What the test requires

You should always ride so that you can stop within the distance you can see to be clear.

Always keep a safe distance between yourself and the vehicle in front.

In good conditions, leave a gap of at least one metre (just over three feet) for every mile per hour you're travelling, or leave a two-second time gap.

In wet conditions, leave at least double the distance, or a four-second time gap.

In slow-moving, congested traffic it may not be practical to leave so much space but the gap should be no less than your thinking distance (see page 52).

## How your examiner will test you

Your examiner will watch carefully and take account of how you

- use the OSM/PSL routine
- anticipate situations
- react to changing road and traffic conditions
- handle the controls.

You should

- be able to judge a safe separation distance between you and the vehicle in front
- show correct use of the OSM/PSL routine, especially before reducing speed
- avoid the need to brake harshly if the vehicle in front slows down or stops
- take extra care when your view ahead is limited by large vehicles such as lorries or buses.

Watch out for

- brake lights ahead
- direction indicators
- vehicles ahead braking without warning.

**Faults to avoid**  You shouldn't

- follow too closely
- brake suddenly
- stop too close to the vehicle in front in a traffic queue.

# Positioning and lane discipline

## What the test requires

You should

- normally keep well to the left
- keep clear of parked vehicles
- avoid weaving in and out between parked vehicles
- position your machine correctly for the direction you intend to take.

You should obey all lane markings, for example, bus and cycle lanes. In one-way streets be particularly aware of left or right turn lane arrows at junctions.

## How your examiner will test you

Your examiner will watch carefully to see that you

- plan ahead and choose the correct lane in good time
- use the OSM/PSL routine correctly
- position your machine sensibly, even if there are no road markings.

**Faults to avoid**  You shouldn't

- ride too close to the kerb or to the centre of the road
- change lanes at the last moment or without good reason
- hinder other road users by being badly positioned or being in the wrong lane
- cut across the path of other traffic in another lane at roundabouts.

*You can't know what's around some corners. Make sure you take up the correct position and ride at a speed where you can stop in the distance that you can see to be clear.*

# Pedestrian crossings

## What the test requires

You should

- recognise the different types of pedestrian crossing
- show courtesy and consideration towards pedestrians
- stop safely when necessary.

## At zebra crossings

You **MUST** slow down and stop if there's anyone on the crossing.

You should also

- slow down and be prepared to stop if there's anyone waiting to cross
- know how to give the correct arm signal, if necessary, before slowing down or stopping.

## At pelican, puffin and toucan crossings

You **MUST**

- stop if the lights are red
- give way to any pedestrians on a pelican crossing when the amber lights are flashing
- give way to cyclists on a toucan crossing, as you would to pedestrians.

## How your examiner will test you

Your examiner will watch carefully and take account of how you deal with pedestrian crossings.

You should be able to

- approach a pedestrian crossing at a controlled speed
- stop safely when necessary
- move off when it's safe, keeping a good look out.

**Faults to avoid** You shouldn't

- approach a crossing too fast
- ride over a crossing without stopping or showing awareness of waiting pedestrians
- block a crossing by stopping on it
- overtake within the zigzag white lines leading up to crossings
- wave pedestrians across
- take late or incorrect action on traffic light signals at controlled crossings.

Don't hurry pedestrians across a crossing by sounding your horn, revving your engine or edging forward.

# Selecting a safe place to stop

## What the test requires

When you make a normal stop you should be able to select a place where you won't obstruct the road or create a hazard. You should pull up close to the edge of the road.

## How your examiner will test you

Your examiner will take account of your use of the OSM/PSL routine and your judgement in selecting a safe place to pull up.

You should know how and where to pull up without causing inconvenience or danger to other road users.

**Faults to avoid**  You shouldn't

- pull up without sufficient warning to other road users
- cause danger or inconvenience to other road users when you pull up.

*Your examiner will ask you to stop in a convenient place. You'll have to choose where to stop and pull up close to the edge of the road.*

# Awareness and anticipation

## What the test requires

You should be aware of other road users at all times. You should

- judge what other road users are likely to do
- predict how their actions will affect you
- react safely and in good time.

You should show awareness of, and consideration for, all other road users. Anticipation of possible danger and concern for safety should also be shown.

*Animals can be unpredictable. Drop your speed and be prepared to stop.*

## How your examiner will test you

**Pedestrians**  Give way to pedestrians when turning from one road to another.

Take particular care with the very young, the disabled and older people. They may misjudge your speed or may not be aware of you.

**Cyclists**  Take special care

- when crossing bus or cycle lanes
- with cyclists passing on your left
- with child cyclists.

**Animals**  Take special care around animals. Give horse riders and other animal handlers as much room as you can. Watch young, possibly inexperienced, riders closely for signs of any difficulty with their mounts. Plan your approach carefully.

**Faults to avoid**  You shouldn't

- react suddenly to road or traffic conditions
- show irritation with other road users
- sound the horn aggressively
- rev your engine or edge forward when waiting for pedestrians or horse riders to cross a road.

# Independent riding

## What the test requires

You should be able to ride independently, making decisions for yourself and planning ahead without instruction, exactly as you will when riding unaccompanied. Look and plan well ahead, taking rear observation as necessary and giving signals correctly and in good time.

If you realise you're taking a wrong turning, you should complete the turn safely as a late sudden change of direction could cause a collision. You'll then need to find somewhere to safely turn around and rejoin your route.

## How your examiner will test you

This section of your test will last around 10 minutes, during which your examiner will ask you to stop in a safe place and will then ask you to

- ride following traffic signs to a destination, or
- follow a series of verbal directions or a combination of both.

Your examiner will be watching how you

- apply the MSM/PSL routine
- plan ahead so that you don't have to make any late actions respond to traffic signs and road markings
- interact with other road users control your motorcycle.

**Faults to avoid**  You shouldn't

- wait until you're at a junction before thinking about which way to turn
- give late or misleading signals
- change lanes at the last moment
- position your motorcycle so that your intention isn't clear
- disobey traffic signs, signals or road markings.

# If you don't pass

## Module 1

Your riding isn't up to the standard required. You didn't complete the specified manoeuvres safely and correctly.

> **Remember,** you'll have to pass Module 1 before you can proceed to Module 2 and you have to pass Module 2 within two years of passing your theory test.

Your examiner will explain the faults and give you a copy of the riding test report.

## Module 2

Your riding isn't up to the standard required. You've made

- serious or dangerous faults
- more than the fixed number of riding faults allowed.

Your examiner will help you by

- giving you a copy of the riding test report. This will show all the faults recorded during the test
- explaining briefly why you haven't passed.

Listen to your examiner carefully. They'll be able to help you by pointing out the aspects of your riding which you need to improve. If you wish, your trainer may be present while your examiner explains why you haven't passed.

Study the riding test report. It will include notes to help you understand how the examiner marks the form. You may then find it helpful to refer to the relevant sections in this book.

If your trainer isn't present during your examiner's explanation, you should show them your copy of the test report. Your trainer will advise and help you to correct the faults. Listen to their advice carefully and get as much practice as you can.

## Right of appeal

You'll obviously be disappointed if you don't pass either module. Although your examiner's decision can't be changed, if you think your test wasn't carried out according to the regulations, you have the right to appeal.

If you live in England and Wales you have six months after the issue of the Statement of Failure in which to appeal (Magistrates' Courts Act 1952 Ch. 55 part VII, Sect. 104).

If you live in Scotland you have 21 days in which to appeal (Sheriff Court, Scotland Act of Sederunt (Statutory Appeals) 1981).

# If you pass both modules

Well done! You'll have shown that you can ride safely.

At the end of Module 2 your examiner will give you a copy of the riding test report. This will show any riding faults which have been recorded during the test and some notes to explain them.

Your examiner will ask for your driving licence so that an upgraded licence can automatically be sent to you through the post. You'll be given a pass certificate (DSA10) as proof of success, until you receive your new full licence.

**Remember,** under the New Drivers Act (see page 123) your licence could be revoked if you receive six or more penalty points within two years of passing your first driving/riding test.

If you don't want to surrender your licence you don't have to, and there will be certain circumstances when this isn't possible, if for example you've changed your name and/or address.

In these cases you'll have to send your provisional licence together with your pass certificate and the appropriate fee to DVLA, and they'll send you your full licence. You have to do this within two years or you'll have to take your test again.

Look at the test report carefully and discuss it with your trainer. It includes notes to help you understand how the examiner marks the form.

You may then find it helpful to refer to the relevant sections in this book to help you overcome weaknesses noted during your test.

## The enhanced rider scheme

DSA, in partnership with training experts and leading insurance companies, has developed a package of training known as the enhanced rider scheme.

The scheme is intended to benefit all motorcycle riders who have a full motorcycle licence, irrespective of riding experience, including those who have just passed their test. Those who undertake further rider development under the scheme will receive considerable insurance discounts from the insurance companies that have signed up to the scheme.

Trainers who deliver the enhanced rider scheme must be registered with DSA on its Register of Post-test Motorcycle Trainers (RPMT).

To find out more about the enhanced rider scheme, or to look for a trainer in your area, visit **www.gov.uk**

# section **six**
# RETESTING

This section covers
- New Drivers Act
- The extended test

# New Drivers Act

Special rules apply for the first two years after the date of passing your first practical test if you held nothing but a provisional licence before passing your test.

## How you may be affected

Your licence will be revoked if the number of penalty points on your licence reaches six or more as a result of offences you commit before the two years are over. This includes offences that you committed before passing your test.

You must then apply for a provisional licence and complete CBT before riding on the road.

You may ride only as a learner until you pass the theory and both modules of the practical test again.

This applies even if you pay by fixed penalty.

*The New Drivers Act was brought in to help keep the roads safer for all road users. Riders who obey the law won't be affected.*

# The extended test

Tough penalties exist for anyone convicted of dangerous driving or riding offences.

Courts must impose an extended test on anyone convicted of such offences.

Courts can also

- impose an extended driving or riding test on anyone convicted of other offences involving obligatory disqualification
- order a normal-length test for other endorsable offences before the disqualified driver or rider can recover a full licence.

*The extended test is assessed to the same standard as the learner test but lasts for about 70 minutes. This makes it more demanding due to the longer time devoted to normal riding.*

## Applying for a retest

A rider subject to a retest can apply for a provisional licence at the end of the disqualification period. CBT must be completed before riding on the road.

The normal rules for provisional licence-holders apply

- L plates (or, if you wish, D plates in Wales) must be displayed to the front and rear of the machine
- solo motorcycles mustn't exceed 125 cc and 11 kW power output (unless riding under the direct access scheme)
- riding on motorways isn't allowed
- pillion passengers may not be carried.

You can book an extended test in the same way as a normal test (see section 3).

## The theory test

You'll have to pass the theory test before an application for the practical test can be made.

Details of the theory test can be found in section 3.

## Longer and more demanding

The extended test takes about 70 minutes and covers a wide variety of roads, usually including dual carriageways. This test is more demanding, so make sure that you're ready.

You're advised to take suitable instruction from an approved motorcycle trainer.

## Higher fees

The higher fee reflects the longer duration of the test.

## How your examiner will test you

Your test will include all off-road and on-road exercises included in the normal test. Your examiner will watch you and take account of

- your ability to concentrate for the duration of the test
- your attitude to other road users.

*At the start of the test you'll have to read and sign a declaration. You're signing to confirm that your machine is suitably insured and also to confirm your UK residency status.*

# section **seven**
# FURTHER INFORMATION

This section covers

- Recommended syllabus

# Recommended syllabus

Riding is a life skill. It will take you many years to acquire the skills set out here to a high standard. This syllabus lists the skills in which you must achieve basic competence. You must also have

- a thorough knowledge of The Highway Code and motoring laws
- an understanding of your responsibilities as a rider.

This means that you must have real concern, not just for your own safety but for the safety of all road users, including pedestrians.

## Legal requirements

To learn to ride on the road, you must

- be aged at least 16 years if you wish to ride a moped, or 17 years if you wish to ride a motorcycle
- be able to read in good daylight (with glasses or contact lenses, if you wear them)
  - a vehicle number plate in the format (XX50XXX) from a distance of 20 metres (about 66 feet)
  - number plates with letters 79.4 mm (3.1 inches) high at a minimum distance of 20.5 metres (about 67 feet)

- be medically fit to hold a licence
- hold a provisional driving licence, or provisional riding entitlement on a full licence for another category
- comply with the requirements of a provisional licence
  - hold a valid compulsory basic training (CBT) certificate
  - display L plates (or, if you wish, D plates in Wales) to the front and rear of the machine
  - pillion passengers mustn't be carried
  - riding on motorways isn't allowed
  - solo motorcycles mustn't exceed 125 cc or 11 kW power output unless learning under the direct access scheme (only open to those over 21 years old), where the machine has a minimum power output of 35 kW (46.6 bhp) and the rider is accompanied by a certified direct access trainer
- ensure that the machine being ridden
  - is legally roadworthy
  - has a current MOT test certificate if it's over three years old
  - displays a valid tax disc
  - is covered by appropriate insurance

- be aware of the legal requirements to declare medical conditions that could affect safe riding. If a machine has been adapted for a disability, ensure that all the adaptations are suitable to control the machine safely
- wear an approved safety helmet correctly fastened when riding a motorcycle on road (members of the Sikh religion who wear a turban are exempt)
- know the rules on the issue, presentation or display of driving licences, insurance certificates, tax discs and CBT certificates.

## Rider safety

You must know

- the safety aspects relating to safety helmets and how to adjust and fasten it correctly
- the safety factors in wearing suitable clothing and using goggles and visors.

## Machine controls, equipment and components

You must

- understand the function of the
  - throttle
  - clutch
  - gears
  - front and rear brakes
  - steering

  and be able to adjust (where applicable) and use these competently

- know the function of all other controls and switches and use them competently
- understand the meaning of the gauges and other displays on the instrument panel
- know the legal requirements for the machine
- be able to carry out routine safety checks such as
  - the brakes for correct operation and cable adjustment or fluid levels
  - the steering head bearings for wear and adjustment
  - fuel, oil and coolant levels
  - tyre pressures
  - chain tension and condition
  - condition of control cables
  - suspension
  - wheels and tightness of nuts and bolts

  and identify defects, especially with the
  - steering
  - brakes
  - tyres
  - lights
  - reflectors
  - direction indicators
  - horn
  - fuel system
  - rear-view mirrors
  - speedometer
  - exhaust system
  - chain

- understand the effect that carrying a load or a pillion passenger will have on the handling of your machine.

## Road user behaviour

You must

- know the most common causes of crashes

- know which road users are most at risk and how to reduce that risk

- know the rules, risks and effects of drinking alcohol and riding

- know the effects of fatigue, illness and drugs on riding performance

- be aware of any age-related problems among other road users, especially among children, teenagers and older people

- be alert and able to anticipate the likely actions of other road users, and be able to take appropriate precautions

- be aware that courtesy and consideration towards other road users are essential for safe riding.

## Machine characteristics

You must

- know the important principles concerning braking distances and road holding under various road and weather conditions

- know the handling characteristics of other vehicles with regard to stability, speed, braking and manoeuvrability

- know that some vehicles are less easily seen than others

- be able to assess the risks caused by the characteristics of other vehicles and suggest precautions that can be taken, for example

  - large commercial vehicles pulling to the right before turning left

  - blind spots for some commercial vehicle drivers

  - bicycles and other motorcyclists being buffeted by strong winds.

## Road and weather conditions

You must

- know the particular hazards in both daylight and darkness, and on different types of road, for example

  - on single carriageways, including country lanes

  - on three-lane roads

  - on dual carriageways and motorways

- gain riding experience on urban and higher-speed roads (but not on motorways) in both daylight and darkness

- know which road surfaces provide the better or poorer grip when braking and cornering

- know the hazards caused by weather conditions, for example
  - bright sunshine
  - rain
  - fog
  - snow
  - ice
  - strong winds
- be able to assess the risks caused by road and traffic conditions, be aware of how the conditions may cause others to drive or ride unsafely, and be able to take appropriate precautions.

## Traffic signs, rules and regulations

You must have a sound knowledge of the meaning of traffic signs and road markings, for example

- speed limits
- parking restrictions
- zebra and pelican crossings.

## Machine control and road procedure

You must have the knowledge and skills to carry out the following tasks safely and competently, practising the proper use of mirrors, observation and signals

- take necessary precautions before mounting or dismounting the machine

- before starting the engine, carry out safety checks on
  - controls
  - mirrors.

  Also check that the gear selector is in neutral
- start the engine and move off
  - straight ahead and at an angle
  - on the level, uphill and downhill
- select the correct road position for normal riding
- use proper observation in all traffic conditions
- be able to carry out the additional safety checks required by riders of motorcycles, for example by
  - using the mirrors
  - looking over the shoulder
  - including the 'lifesaver' check
- be able to use the front and rear brakes correctly
- know how to lean while cornering, tested at a minimum speed of 30 km/h (about 19 mph) during the off-road module of the test
- ride at a speed suitable for road and traffic conditions
- react promptly to all risks
- change traffic lanes
- pass stationary vehicles
- meet, overtake and cross the path of other vehicles

- turn right and left at junctions, including crossroads and roundabouts

- ride ahead at crossroads and roundabouts

- keep a safe separation distance when following other traffic

- act correctly at pedestrian crossings

- show proper regard for the safety of other road users, with particular care towards the most vulnerable

- ride on both urban and rural roads and, where possible, dual carriageways – keeping up with the flow of traffic where it's safe and proper to do so

- comply with traffic regulations and traffic signals given by the police, traffic officers, traffic wardens and other road users

- steer the machine to avoid a stationary obstacle at a minimum speed of 50 km/h (about 32 mph), tested during the off-road module of the test

- stop the machine safely, normally and in an emergency, without locking the wheels, tested at a minimum speed of 50 km/h (about 32 mph) during the off-road module of the test

- be able to ride a U-turn safely

- be able to keep the machine balanced at slow speeds and while steering

- be able to wheel the machine, without the aid of the engine, while walking alongside it

- be able to park and remove the machine from its stand

- cross all types of railway level crossing.

## Additional knowledge

You must know

- the importance of correct tyre pressures

- the action needed to avoid and correct skids

- how to ride through floods and flooded areas

- what to do if you're involved in a crash or breakdown, including the special arrangements for crashes or breakdowns on a motorway

- basic first aid for use on the road as set out in The Highway Code

- how to deter motorcycle thieves.

## Motorway riding

You must gain a sound knowledge of the special rules, regulations and riding techniques for motorway riding before taking your practical riding test.

After passing your test, further training is recommended with a motorcycle trainer before riding unsupervised on motorways.

See page 121 for information on DSA's enhanced rider scheme.

# Other official DSA publications

From the Driving Standards Agency –
the official route to Safe Riding for Life™

Driving
Standards
Agency

## For learners

### The Official DSA Theory Test for Motorcyclists

Packed with official theory test revision questions and background information to help you really understand.

**Book**
ISBN 9780115532344 £14.99

**Downloadable PDF\***
ISBN 9780115532351 £14.99

**DVD-ROM**
ISBN 9780115532610 £12.99

**Interactive download**
ISBN 9780115531989 £9.99

### The Official DSA Guide to Hazard Perception

Develop your hazard perception skills and learn more about this part of the theory test.

**Interactive DVD**
ISBN 9780115528651 £15.99

*\*for instant access from tsoshop.co.uk*

  **safedrivinglife**

**@safedrivinglife**

## For all bikers

### The Official DSA Guide to Riding – the essential skills

Packed with advice for learners and all motorcyclists.

**Book**
ISBN 9780115532467 £12.99

**Downloadable PDF\***
ISBN 9780115532474 £12.99

### Better Biking – the official DSA training aid

Help to improve your riding skills and information about the enhanced rider scheme.

**DVD**
ISBN 9780115529559 £10.99

Also available with The Official DSA Theory Test for Motorcyclists DVD-ROM in The Official DSA Biker Pack.
ISBN 9780115532634 £19.99

Buy official DSA titles and view the full range at **tsoshop.co.uk/dsa** or call **0870 850 6553**. Also available from all good high street book stores.

## Rules of the road

### The Official Highway Code

Essential reading for all road users.

**Book**
ISBN 9780115528149 £2.50

**Interactive CD-ROM**
ISBN 9780115528460 £9.99

**British Sign Language pack**
ISBN 9780115529849 £9.99

**eBook**
Also available from your device's eBook store.

### Official Highway Code iPhone app

All the rules of the road at your fingertips and quizzes to test your knowledge. Available on the iPhone app store.

### Awarded to The Official Highway Code range in 2012.

Prince Michael
**INTERNATIONAL ROAD SAFETY AWARD**

*Recognising achievement and innovations which will improve road safety*

# The **OFFICIAL DSA GUIDE to**
# LEARNING
## to Ride

# 2013 WIN
# BIKE GEAR
# COMPETITION

**TSO, DSA's official publishing partner, is offering you the chance to win new motorcycle clothing or accessories.***

To enter, simply answer the questions and tell us in 25 words or less how learning to ride will make a difference to your life. The winner will be the entrant who answers the first three questions correctly and writes the most apt and original 25-word tie breaker, as decided by the judges. Closing date: 31 December 2013.

**Please send the entry form to:**
Win Bike Gear Competition 2013, TSO, Freepost, ANG 4748, Norwich, NR3 1YX (no stamp required).

1. **What is the minimum motorcycle engine size allowed on a motorway?**

..................................................................................................................................

2. **What is the legal minimum depth of tread for motorcycle tyres in millimetres?**

..................................................................................................................................

3. **You hold a provisional motorcycle licence. When are you allowed to carry a pillion passenger?**

..................................................................................................................................

**Tie Breaker: Learning to ride will change my life.... (complete in 25 words or less)**

..................................................................................................................................

..................................................................................................................................

..................................................................................................................................

\* Terms and conditions apply

**Name of shop or website that you bought this product from?**

.......................................................................................................................

**Why did you choose this particular product?**

.......................................................................................................................

.......................................................................................................................

**How would you improve this, or any other DSA product?**

.......................................................................................................................

.......................................................................................................................

.......................................................................................................................

Name .................................................................................................................

Address ..............................................................................................................

.................................................................... Date of birth ..............................

Daytime telephone number ..............................................................................

Mobile telephone number ..................................................................................

Email ..................................................................................................................
TSO would like to continue to keep you informed of products and services that may be of interest to you. If you do not wish to receive these updates in future please let us know.

☐ I do not want to receive these updates from TSO in future

*I have read, accept and agree to be bound by the Competition Rules*

Signature ............................................................. Date ..............................

If you would like us to send you email updates on your specific area(s) of interest register at tsoshop.co.uk/signup.

# Competition Rules

**The following rules apply to this competition. By entering this competition, entrants will be deemed to have accepted these rules and to agree to be bound by them.**

1. Only one entry will be accepted per purchase of The Official DSA Guide to Learning to Ride.
2. All entries must be on original official entry forms. No photocopies will be accepted.
3. Entries must be received by the Promoter by no later than 5.00pm on Tuesday, 31 December 2013 (**Closing Date**). Entries must be submitted by ordinary post to the Promoter's free mailing address at: TSO, Freepost, ANG 4748, Norwich, NR3 1YX.
4. The competition will run from 10 September 2012 to 31 December 2013 and one prize shall be awarded to a winner chosen from valid entries received by the Promoter by the Closing Date. No responsibility can be taken by the Promoter for lost, late, misdirected or stolen entries.
5. The prize awarded to the winner will be a range of bike clothing to a value of approximately £1000 (at the time of these rules going to press (Prize)). The Promoter may in its absolute discretion substitute this Prize with a similar prize of approximate equivalent value. There will be one Prize only and accordingly only one winner. Prizes cannot be transferred or exchanged and there is no cash alternative.
6. Only entrants over the age of 16 and resident in the United Kingdom are eligible to enter the competition. The Promoter reserves the right to request evidence of proof of age and residence from the winner before any prize will be awarded.
7. The winning entry will be decided by the judges in their absolute discretion from correct entries submitted by eligible entrants received by the Closing Date. A "correct" entry means a fully completed entry, with the first three questions answered correctly, the most apt and original essay and otherwise in compliance with these rules.
8. The winner will be notified by 22 January 2014. Only the winner will be contacted personally via the email address or telephone number they provide.
9. If the winner cannot be contacted by the means provided, the Promoter reserves the right to have the judges decide on an alternative winner from other correct entries received by the Closing Date, using the same criteria as for the original "winner" and subject to these rules.
10. The winner's name will be published on the Promoter's website at tso.co.uk on or about 1 February 2014 for a period of approximately 60 days.
11. The prize will be made available within six weeks of the Closing Date by arrangement between the Promoter and the winner, provided that the Promoter shall not be responsible for any delivery costs.
12. By entering this competition, an entrant agrees they will be deemed to consent to the use for promotional and other purposes (without further payment and except as prohibited by law) of their name, city/town/county of residence and competition entry, including any opinions or comments provided; an entrant, if they accept any Prize further agree they will be deemed to consent to:
    (a)     the use for promotional and other purposes (without further payment and except as prohibited by law) of their likeness;
    (b)     participate in the Promoter's reasonable marketing and promotional activities.
    The entrant agrees that all rights including copyright in all works created by the entrant as part of the competition entry shall be owned by the Promoter absolutely without the need for any payment to the entrant. They further agree to waive unconditionally and irrevocably all moral rights pursuant to the Copyright, Designs and Patents Act of 1988 and under any similar law in force from time to time anywhere in the world in respect of all such works.
13. No entries will be returned to entrants by the Promoter. Therefore, entrants may wish to retain a copy.
14. The Promoter reserves the right to cancel this competition or amend these rules at any stage without prior notice, if deemed necessary in its opinion, especially if circumstances arise outside of its control. Any such cancellation or changes to the rules will be notified on the Promoter's website.
15. This competition is not open to employees or contractors of the Promoter or the Driving Standards Agency or any person directly involved in the organisation or running of the competition, or their direct family members. Any such entries will be invalid.
16. By entering this competition, entrants warrant that all information submitted by them is true and correct and that they are eligible and have legal capacity to enter this competition. The Promoter reserves the right to disqualify any entrant if it has reasonable grounds to believe that the entrant has breached these rules.
17. Any personal data provided in any entry will be dealt with by the Promoter in accordance with the requirements of the Data Protection Act 1998, provided that the winner expressly consents to the information set out in rule 12(a) being used in the manner specified therein.
18. The judges' and the Promoter's decisions in relation to any aspect of this competition are final and no correspondence will be entered into. Neither the judges nor the Promoter will have any liability to any person in relation to their decisions or any damage, loss, injury or disappointment suffered arising from the competition (except to the extent that such liability cannot be limited or excluded by law).
19. The competition and these rules shall be governed by English law.
20. The "Promoter" means The Stationery Office Limited, St Crispins, Duke Street, Norwich, NR3 1PD (the publishers of The Official DSA Learner Range). The competition judging panel will be made up of a combination of the Promoter's employees and independent judge(s).

Driving
Standards
Agency

# Learning to ride?

Remember to prepare for your theory and practical tests using the official materials for expert information from the people who set the tests. For the full range of DSA titles go to **tsoshop.co.uk/dsa**

Did you know you can:

- book your theory test
- book your practical test

and much more by visiting:

# www.gov.uk

or call customer services on 0300 200 1122

 **Join the conversation**

Questions about learning to ride? Follow **@Liz_DSA @John_DSA @Linda_DSA**

Keep up-to-date with the latest rules of the road **@HighwayCodeGB**

 Find out what to expect when you take your theory and practical motorcycle tests:
**youtube.com/dsagov**

 **start2ride**

Scan to become a fan for hints, tips and news for learners
*(you'll need a phone with a QR code reader app to read the code)*

**HighwayCodeGB**

Find out about all the latest rules of the road